DIASPORA·ISH

notes on
Identities, Unbelonging,
& Solidarities

Gayatri Sethi

New York | An imprint of Sambasivan & Parikh

DIASPORA·ISH
Notes on Identities, Unbelonging, & Solidarities

Text © 2026 by Gayatri Sethi.

All rights reserved.
No part of this book may be reproduced in any form whatsoever, by photography or xerography or by any other means, by broadcast or transmission, by translation into any kind of language, nor by recording electronically or otherwise, without permission in writing from the publisher, except by a reviewer, who may quote brief passages in critical articles or reviews.

Without in any way limiting the author's and publisher's exclusive rights under copyright, any use of this publication to train generative artificial intelligence (AI) technologies to generate text or art is expressly prohibited.

Published in the United States of America by First Person Press, an imprint of Sambasivan & Parikh.

ISBN: 978-1-949528-05-3
978-1-949528-04-6 (Hardcover)
978-1-949528-06-0 (eBook)

Book typeset in Freight.

Editing by Mitali Desai.
Cover and book design by Annika Sarin.

"So often, children of diaspora unlearn oppressive narratives in isolation from one another. We unlearn them through cycles of error, harm, and forgiveness. We forge a path different from that of our ancestors, and pass the knowledge we gain on to our children, hoping that they choose solidarity over exceptionalism from the outset. In *Diaspora-ish*, Gayatri Sethi has codified her own unlearning, and made it an offering to all of us. How lucky are the daughters of diaspora to have this book on our shelves as a companion on their journeys of unlearning and relearning. How lucky are we all to have *Diaspora-ish* as an intergenerational learning resource for our collective struggle and solidarity."—**Neema Avashia, author of** *Another Appalachia: Coming Up Queer and Indian in a Mountain Place*

"In this groundbreaking collection, Sethi explores topics such as identity and belongingness to not only raise questions about what it means to be in community with each other, but also help those who constantly feel as though they don't belong, feel seen and accepted."
—**Dr. Rita Shah, Professor of Criminology, Eastern Michigan University**

"More than a book, *Diaspora-ish* is a call to action, a challenge to reconsider our place in the world, and interrogate our very way of thinking. A powerful and timely read."—**Adiba Jaigirdar, award-winning author of** *The Henna Wars*

"In *Diaspora-ish*, author and educator Gayatri Sethi insightfully examines how identity shapes belonging, as well as how both can become double-edged swords in service of insidious imperial systems. Using the same genre-bending, multimedia style as her powerful debut *Unbelonging*, Sethi wields an incisive blend of prose and poetry that challenges readers to reflect—often directly within the pages of the book—on the pretty, perilous traps identity politics can lure us into, while also teaching us how to begin the process of liberating ourselves and our comrades. If you truly believe that none of us are free until all of us are free—if you genuinely want to decolonize and emancipate yourself from empire—*Diaspora-ish* is a must read."—**Priyanka Taslim, author of** *The Love Match* **and** *Always Be My Bibi*

"Powerful and poignant, Dr Sethi's book is not just genre-defying, but also identity-defying. It will not just encourage quiet reflection, but also powerful rebellion and solidarity. Dr. Gayatri Sethi's verse offers a tool kit to unlearning and learning, unbelonging and belonging. *Diaspora-ish* is an empowering read I recommend reading and re- reading. I look forward to more books from this talented author!"
—**Reem Faruqi, author of** *Unsettled* **and** *Zarina Divided*

"*Diaspora-ish*'s call to embrace "open heart living" in a time when all things related to immigration, identity, and diaspora are being acutely criminalized is an invitation back to our humanity. The author invites us into criticality with curiosity, hope, self-awareness, and radical love, so that we may challenge dominant, oppressive narratives about who belongs and why. ¡En solidaridad, siempre!" —**Dr. Ivania Delgado, Clinical Assistant Professor and Practicum Director of MSW at Saint Joseph's University**

"*Diaspora-ish* puts into words what so many of us have been experiencing, wrestling with, suppressing for so many years. I have to sit with each page. Meditate. Feel it."—**Safa Suleiman, educator and author of** *Hilwa's Gifts*

"Gayatri Sethi's voice is essential, especially in a time when so many communities live outside their homelands, when the question of home is so fraught with complexities. In these pages, we learn what it means to truly embrace and act in solidarity with others who become our anchors and—in the highest meaning of the word—our kin."—**Susan Muaddi Darraj, award-winning author of** *Behind You Is the Sea*

"*Diaspora-ish* is a deeply poetic touchstone for those turning their minds, hearts and actions toward collective liberation. A must-have."
—**Karuna Riazi, author of** *A Bit of Earth* **and** *Sabrena Swept Away*

For the diasporic who seek belonging and find liberations in unbelonging. Y'all keep our collective solidarities alive.

Care Notes

The following pages include mentions & explorations of these themes:

Colonialism & imperialism

History of partition & displacement

Systems of oppression

Racism & anti-Blackness

Patriarchy & misogyny

Casteism

Trauma & abuse

Interpersonal violence

Homophobia & transphobia

Contents

Foreword	viii
Letter to the Reader	x
Reading Guide	xii
IDENTITIES	15
DESI·ISH	33
AFRICAN·ISH	77
African-ish Geographies	81
African-ish Histories	86
African-ish Ways	105
EMIGRATION	119
AMERICAN·ISH	129
Immigrations	134
Educations	149
Identities and Unbelongings	159
SOLIDARITIES	205
Unlearning and Learning	208
Collective Dreaming	216
Solidarity ... Solidarities	225
REVOLUTIONS	231
APPENDIX	245

For those ready to do aatma da kam:

This book is a constellation—multilingual, multimodal, multicultural, multifaith, multigeographical. It carries many worlds inside it, refusing to belong to just one. It is part poetry, part workbook, part journal, part invitation. A breathing, moving text that does not let you simply read it; it asks you to live it. It is for those ready to do aatma da kam, soul work: that brave, bruising labor of looking within and asking, who am I in this world, and who do I become in the worlds I help create?

Through verse and reflection, it gathers the voices of scholars, activists, revolutionaries—voices too often silenced or erased from the main stage of literature and public memory. In these pages, they speak again. Their words hum with history, grief, resistance, and rebirth. They remind us that critique is an act of care—that to question society, we must first question ourselves.

This is not a passive read. The text demands your pause. It interrupts your scrolling, your skimming, your easy comfort. It inserts breath breaks and reflection spaces, turning the act of reading into ritual. Each section calls you back to your own life, to your classrooms, to your communities. It insists that what happens on the page must echo in practice.

In the midst of apocalyptic feelings—this sense that everything is crumbling, because it is—the book whispers: maybe the breaking is part of the healing, part of the making. It is a guide for future dreaming, for paradigm shifting, for worldbuilding that can happen in the diaspora, in the here and now. It names what is painful and what is possible, what we must dismantle and what we must dare to imagine.

This book is both balm and mirror. It critiques culture and policy with precision and love. It does not leave out the ugly, the horrible, the hard—because truth-telling is its own kind of tenderness. It holds space for rage and for rest, for mourning and for movement.

For those at the beginning of their activism journey, this is not a "how-to." It is a "here('s)/why." A reminder that the revolution begins inside heads, homes, and in the hearts, before it takes to the streets. It is poetic, cutting-edge, and critical—a text that holds the tension between beauty and brutality, hope and honesty.

To read this book is to be seen, unsettled, and set in motion.
This is not a book you finish—
      it lingers.
it's a book you return to, again and again,
as you build a better self, a better society,
a better future.

Victoria Gill, Ed.D.
Assistant Professor, Lesley University

Beloved reader,

Who am I? Where do I belong? Who are my people?

For much of my life, I have grappled with these fundamentally human questions. But as a descendant of people who were made refugees, as a child to immigrants born in Tanzania, and as an immigrant myself to north america, these inquiries have often been aggravated by life experiences of exclusion, discrimination, and othering. As I talk to folks of multiple generations, I realize that what so many of us consider a personal "identity crisis" might be a shared experience of living in diaspora.

During times of upheaval characterized by climate disaster, social injustices, humanitarian catastrophes, and genocides, our sense of self and each other is all the more in question. Many of us are braving highly uncertain presents and futures.

In my ongoing search for answers, and ways of connecting my experiences to larger collective understandings, I began writing the words in this book. A few years ago, in a previous iteration of musings and reflections titled *Unbelonging*, I proposed that we normalize not belonging. What if we accepted that some of us, no matter where we go or where we try to fit in, simply do not belong? In this new book, I extend my thinking and search for explanations to include ongoing learning about identity and solidarity.

Rather than writing formal prose or an academic-style text about these themes, this is an experimental, genre-defiant book. Many entries and pages take the form of journal-like entries of observations and inquiries. My aim is to invite readers to engage with the issues within using reflective and critical thinking. I include repeated invitations to unlearn, learn, and relearn what we have been taught about ourselves, each other, and the world we inhabit.

Perhaps, we might need to rethink our inquiries. Who are we? Why do we seek to belong? With whom do we rebuild solidarity? How do we unmake this world in revolutionary ways?

I invite you, beloved reader, to enter the ensuing pages bravely with an open heart and mind. It is my radical hope that what you read may shift your thinking, feeling, and being, too. I embrace you with care as you embark on this relearning journey.

In earnest solidarity,

Gayatri

Reading Guide

A few suggestions as you read this book

This book is intended to be an interactive, brave space of reflection, healing, and creation. Many holistic educators believe that learning is healing. True learning shifts us from discomfort to understanding by engaging our heads, hearts, and hands.

ENGAGE

The words and illustrations herein are created to evoke a warm embrace even as you might feel new emotions and be challenged by some of these uncomfortable truths. It is my earnest hope that you will experience this book actively. Try this: Highlight words. Doodle in the margins. Scratch out words. Fold the pages if you are so inclined. Add your own ideas. Write your own reflections in the margins or blank spaces. Express yourself!

UNLEARN

This book is designed by an educator to facilitate learning. Use the prompts and inquiries to self-reflect. Create space to process your own observations and experiences related to these themes. Passive reading does not result in shifts in understanding. When you feel emotionally provoked by ideas you encounter, pause. Regular spaces and reflection prompts are included to facilitate processing of thoughts and emotions. Take your time.

LEARN

Research and invitations for further study are embedded throughout. When you encounter a new word or phrase, circle it and add it to the inquiries and notes pages embedded throughout the book. The transition pages from each subsection to the next are replete with learning resources in the form of inquiries, citations, and key concepts. You are encouraged to dig deeper into the concepts highlighted in the invitations to research. There are fields of study and well-known authors and scholars whose ideas informed this work. They are cited and named throughout. Create your own learning and reading lists.

RELEARN

New concepts and forms are included herein. You will encounter new languages, scripts, and symbols. Certain reframes and departures from writing convention, even capitalizations and spellings, are deliberate. Consider the reasons underlying these efforts. Release attachments to widely accepted communication norms while reading. Reimagine the power of language. Revise your communications intentionally.

SHARE

This book is designed to be a multifaceted learning experience— equal parts poetry collection, workbook, and journal. If these words, verses, and inquiries provoke new understandings or actions, feel free to create your own art in these pages and outside them. Start a conversation. Share the book's ideas with your circle of friends and community. Form a book club. Plan a teach-in or workshop. Collaborate on new possibilities for relearning in collectives.

Identities

Why identify?

Identity matters.
We see color.
We are not invisible.
We are not ether.

Race is a construction
and race has real life ramifications.

Name all the intersections.
If we do not say who we are,
if we do not claim all our selves,
we will be erased.

We need to see how we are differently placed
before we can claim to all be one human race.

Identify.

What is identity?

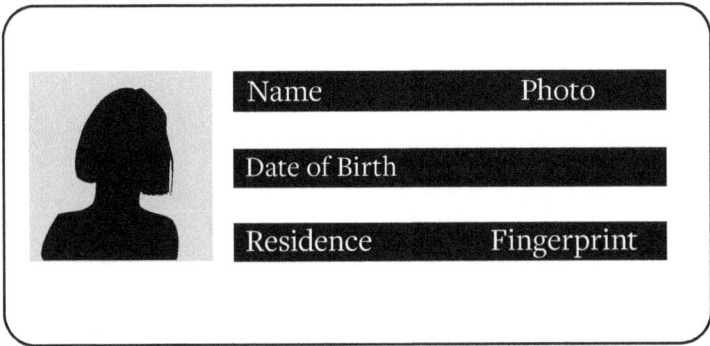

Have you ever wondered why forms of identification like passports exist & for what purpose?

What am I?

Identity Categories
Enter words you identify with when you are completing demographic forms.

- ☐ Race _____
- ☐ Ethnicity _____
- ☐ Age _____
- ☐ Gender _____
- ☐ Sexuality _____
- ☐ Religion _____
- ☐ Caste _____
- ☐ Class _____
- ☐ Nationality _____

Are you still at a loss when you are asked identity questions?

I rarely respond with words (*mostly feels*) when asked questions and inquiries that land like blows, weapons even.

What are you? (*sarcasm or silence*)
Who are you? (*humor or hurt*)
Where are you from? (*defensiveness or digression*)
Why are you here? (*deflection or dismay*)

Unbox me

We are expected to check boxes
but who lives in boxes?
This or that?
Here or there?
Pick one box.
Check it.

☒ I am other.
☒ I am also all of the above.
☒ Am I everything?

A wise poet oft quoted says,
I contain multitudes.
Truer words I never heard said
about myself.
We cannot be contained
in boxes or closets or binaries.

Humans are fluid.

I flow in the gaps.
I live in the intersections.

I live in the
   margins.

I even inhabit the margins of the intersections.
   I cannot be divided or carved up into sections.
   I cannot check a box.

   I would be split
   on the atomic level
   and then everything else,
   like the box,
   would **explode**.

Identity struggle song

Who am I?

Who on earth am I?

Frantz Fanon says, "In the world through which i travel, i am endlessly creating myself."[1]

---

1. Frantz Fanon, *Black Skin, White Masks* (Grove Press, Inc., 1967), 229.

Words matter. Names matter.

those who look at me but do not know me throw around these words:

immigrant

brown

woman of color　　**other**　　**migrant**

bipoc　　**south asian**　　**desi**

proud

　　　opinionated

　　　　　　condescending　　　outspoken

threatening　　confusing

　　　　　　　　　　woke

　　　　　　crazy　　　　　　articulate

　angry

　　　　defiant　　　　exotic

　　　　　　foreign

disgraceful

　　　　　　　　　　　　　divisive

　　　　disruptive

do they know me?
do they even see me?

thank heavens i know myself enough
to not be limited, constrained,
or contained
by words that are not
my own.

names matter. words matter.

Words they call me

those who know me call me: **mama** aunty bua teacher professor masi friend mentor scholar sister dada fam kin beti didi bibi

gayatri

they say: **you are honest** a truth-teller fearless safe kind protector knower insightful wise fierce a revolutionary one of us.

Naming is healing

Politicians threaten to "send us back."
People demand, "Go back to where you came from."
Identity can be weaponized.

for those of us who are wounded by weaponized unbelonging
even by those who share identities with us,
there is a deep healing power in learning to name and identify ourselves.

Words to describe our character are not the same as our identity.

What not?

Audre Lorde said, "If i didn't define myself for myself, i would be crunched into other people's fantasies for me and eaten alive."[2]

Define me not
by what I am not.
You call me non-white.
You refer to us as non-Europeans.
You tell us we are non-English speakers.
I do not define myself as what not.
I deny dominance of what I am not.

Question identity

No matter the inquiry, i am other.

---

2. Audre Lorde, "Learning from the 60s," in *Sister Outsider: Essays and Speeches* (Crossing Press, 1984), 137.

How about asking, how do you identify?

Leave the responses open-ended.

Symptoms of unbelonging: a self-diagnosis

Longing Discomfort Sabotage Malaise Insecurity Anxiety
Mania Paranoia Wanderlust Fernweh Meraki Eunoia Ataraxia
Hodophilia Be/longing

Human | بشر | इंसान | Humaine

I am 100% human
striving to be humane
seeking to cultivate humanity.

Will this ever be enough?
When will this be enough?
Where on earth will this be enough?

Belonging struggle song

Where do I belong?

Where on earth do I belong?

Why struggle with identity & belonging?
Around the globe,
hate crimes are proliferating.

I am diaspora-ish.

Diaspora

What is the word for someone
who cannot define a single identity
or origin?
What is the word to identify someone
who cannot define a single place they belong?
What is the word that defies definition
to mean someone is from nowhere
and everywhere?
Is it diaspora?
Not quite, but maybe.
Diaspora is neither an identity nor a geography.

-ish?

To be -ish
is to be multi-identified
& this is to be this & that & that
& that too all at once.
To be -ish is to be &
never either/or
but ever & &.
I say I am "ish" when speaking about my identitites.
I belong and unbelong.

What if I becomes i?

Gayatri Sethi

Send me back?

Beware if you attempt to "send me back" you
will have to piece me up.
Partition me. Into multitudes.
Send my head in parts to all the lands and places
where I've lived and learned.

But how much of my head will you keep here in
this land called america?
As I have studied and labored and taught at places of higher learning
built on the land whose original keepers are the Yurok, Muscogee,
and Illini.

Send my heart to the Lake Nyanza (Victoria) region of Tanzania
where I was born.
Send my hands to the land that is now known as Pakistan where my
ancestors were born two generations ago.
Send my insides to India, Punjab—
where my people have resided after Partition.

Send an organ of your choosing to Iran, the
birthplace of a faith I follow.
Another to Palestine, holy land of many faiths
we follow.

They might return it to the sender.

Beware if you try to send me back you must send me to
Botswana where I was raised,
where my passport says I am a citizen.

Send my feet to all the lands and places I've
traveled and sojourned—too many to name—from Aruba to Cuba to
France to Mauritius to Trinidad to Zimbabwe.

DIASPORA·ISH

Won't you please send tiny pieces of me to
everywhere I've felt at home and at peace?
The Caribbean and Mediterranean Seas.
The Indian and Atlantic Oceans.
Keep my uterus in america
because it held and birthed
american children.
This land is rightfully theirs—despite all the denial—as their paternal
people are descended from those enslaved by this land's settlers.

Their ancestors built this land.
They were raised to respect this stolen land.

If I leave my american children here—the most precious parts of
me—
I dread and fear
you will discard or exile them, too,
as you disown their immigrant parent.

Perhaps, I will take my progeny with me
to lands still unknown where we will know no fear
because of the colors of our skin,
our worship, practices, our names.

Beware if you attempt to send me back,
partition me piece by piece, too
many pieces, traces of me
will be left behind in america's soil.

How will you erase or recompense me
for the cumulative impact of my existence here?

As my soul is indivisible, she will roam unshackled and borderless
wherever she pleases.
Send me back?
Piece by piece, yet

I will remain intact.

Notes

Reflection Invitation:

What are your working definitions of and connections between the following terms or concepts?

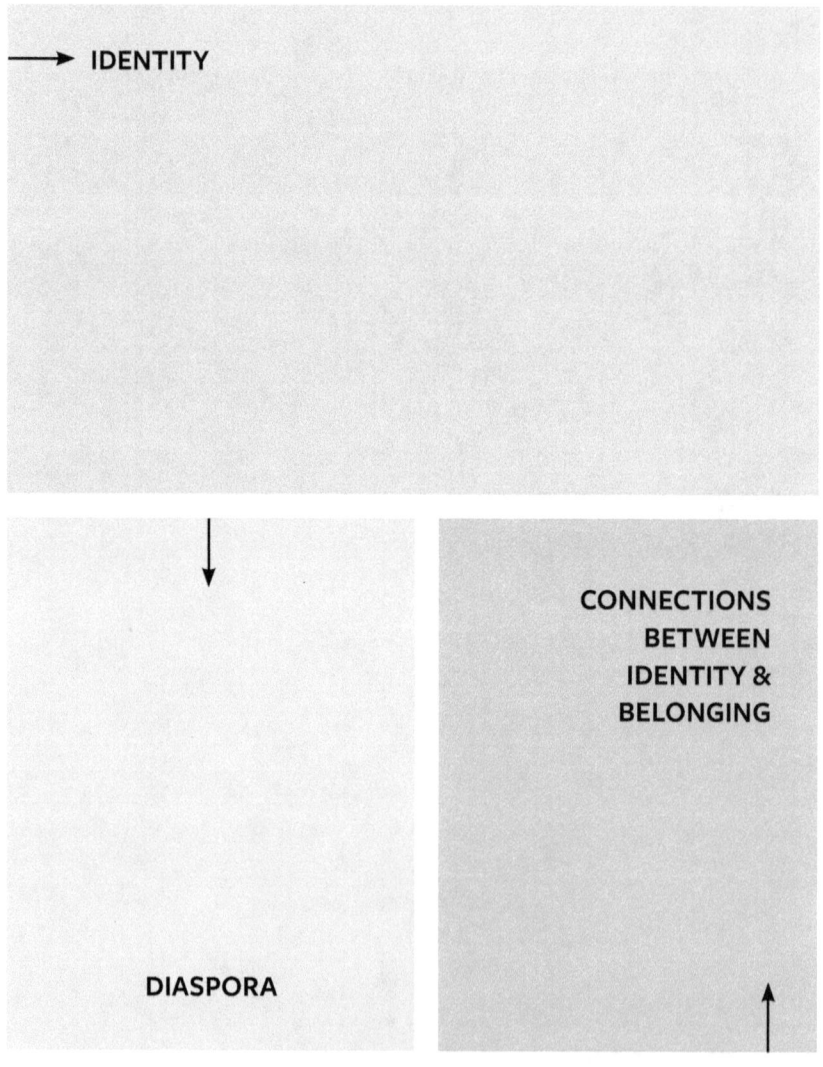

Gayatri Sethi

BELONGING

CULTURE

DISTINCTION BETWEEN IDENTITY
POLITICS & IDENTITY REDUCTIONISM

Inquiries

Why does identity matter?

Janet Mock says, "There is a power in naming yourself, in proclaiming to the world that this is who you are."[3]

What are the origins of identity categories like race, gender, caste & class? What are distinctions between class & caste; race & ethnicity; gender & sexuality?

Edward Said taught us, "No one today is purely one thing. Labels like Indian, or woman, or Muslim, or American are not more than starting points, which if followed into actual experience for only a moment are quickly left behind. Imperialism consolidated the mixture of cultures and identities on a global scale."[4]

⇒

---

[3]. Janet Mock, *Redefining Realness: My Path to Womanhood, Identity, Love & So Much More* (Atria Books, 2014), 85.

[4]. Edward W. Said, *Culture and Imperialism* (Vintage Books, 1994), 336.

How do we rethink identity?

Stuart Hall reflected, "I came to understand that identity is not a set of fixed attributes, the unchanging essence of the inner self, but a constantly shifting process of positioning . . . In fact, identity is always a never-completed process of becoming—a process of shifting identifications, rather than a singular, complete, finished state of being."[5]

---

5. Stuart Hall with Bill Schwarz, *Familiar Stranger: A Life Between Two Islands* (Duke University Press, 2017), 16.

DESI•ISH

Are you?

are you indian? no.
are you south asian? sort of.
are you south asian american? not quite.
are you asian? depends.
are you indo-african? maybe.
are you desi? Desi-ish.

Desi-ish

Desi signifies origins in the
South Asian subcontinent.
It is a contested & yet
expansive way to self-identify.
Some folks avoid or shun the
identifier entirely.
i experiment & play with it.

i am desi-ish
because i do not have any other words to convey the
complex diasporic perpetual immigration
unbelonging
story that unravels in me and around me.

i say i am desi-ish because
although i trace my lineage to punjab,
i was not born or raised there.
my mother pined for her desh with
the deep patriotic longing that i
acknowledge in her without feeling
myself.

to be born away from the desh is
to speak its tongues, understand its
words, and still seek meaning.
it is to seek your heritage, love
your origins,
while resisting imposed parameters of
belonging.

> *what does it mean to be desi-ish?*
> *it is to ever know but not know.*
> *it is to belong but defy.*
> *it is to understand but resist.*

Who am I?

I'm a hyphenated human.
I'm adept at adapting where I go.
I'm a polyglot.
Malleable.
I speak many tongues.
I have numerous personas.
I make myself at home, but I'm not sure where I belong.
Some days, my hyphens and parentheses erase me.
For all of this, I'm judged.
I'm judged harshly for being inauthentic. Fake. Condescending.
Too much this. Not enough that.
Do you judge me because you don't understand me?

Identity. Who am I?

Who I am is always in flux.
Keeping up with who I am and who I become has always been my quest.
Who am I?
In my moments of clarity, I remember.
In my moments of angst and despair, I don't quite know.
My identity has been policed.
All my life somebody has tried to tell me who I'm not.
You're not Indian.
Your Hindi sounds foreign, like childish talk.
You're not Tanzanian.
Your Kiswahili and birth certificate don't prove you belong here.
Lekgoa, they call me in Botswana.
Lekgoa?
But, I am not a white person who has money.
We are humble and brown.
Aren't we?
Futsek. Go back to where you came from.
Where is that exactly?
I came to america.
Naively thinking I'd find myself here.
They asked me, "What are you?"
Neither Black nor white.
Foreigner. Immigrant. Other.

Neither here nor there.
Claim my Indian self?
The desis mocked my "African" and western ways.
"I wasn't raised in India," I said.
"But I do speak Hindi and understand Punjabi and Gujarati.
My extended family still lives there.
I used to visit."
(Eye roll. Dismissed.)

But they're right.
I defied their Indian ways.
I didn't want to be a subservient girl who passively accepted roles assigned to her.
I despised caste discrimination.
Classism and anti-Blackness made me rage.
Arranged marriage? No, thanks.

Who am I?

I'm the one who proves I can. I'll defy. I resist.
I've always had this fire in me.
I married who I loved.
I defied the race boundaries.
Knowing more walls and separations would come from this choice.
"He's African american. That's just not done.
No Indian girl ought to shame her community that way."
Wait a minute.

You police me, but say I am not desi enough. The desi
card was never mine. So why fuss now?
What business of yours is it who I marry or why?
We disown you. We block you. We stonewall you.
Indian? I wasn't born in India.
I'm not African. I was born there.
I'm not american though I sometimes speak and act like I am.
My children are (Indian)-African-american.
We are punctuated with hyphens and parentheses.
I'm not sure what goes before or after my hyphens.
Some parts of me remain hidden in parentheses. (. . .)

Who am I?

What are some ways of identifying people?

My name is . . .

i was blessed with a distinctly desi name.
gayatri.
gayatri is a mantra.
it is sacred.
gayatri is a deity.
she is the embodiment
of transcendent knowledge.
she represents the knowing that defies
rationality
and invites spirituality.

i do not fully understand how
a brown child born on african soil,
to a father who relinquished his hindu identity
to embrace a faith associated with islam by his hindu kin,
was given such a name.

how did my parent who did not press his
palms together, but rather invoked allah,
palms open to the heavens,
name me after a hindu deity and a
mantra
he rarely chanted?
this is the conundrum of my name,
and so it rarely conveys my own sense of me.

My not-so indian self

i had a dream in which someone asked me, "what's up with you and india?"
i replied that i'm one of her alienated daughters
seeking reconciliation.

i haven't visited since i was eighteen.
my pa bought me a ticket and sent me solo as a precondition to going to college in the u.s.
he predicted i wouldn't go on my own.
he had a way of just knowing. memories are fleeting.

i cherish the conversations i had with my mataji while shelling peas, marveling at her slow and gentle ways. i chuckle at the shenanigans with my cousins. i smile thinking of the meals with buas and uncles, forty or more of us talking and eating all at once in one tight space.

growing up on another continent, we didn't have such festivity. we didn't have history together like this. we didn't quite fit. we spoke hindi and heard punjabi (how we managed this while growing up on african soil is a feat unto itself), but our accents made everyone laugh.

to be desi-ish is
to be uprooted and replanted so often that
one sprouts wings from the unearthed roots.

every human in every hue who policed my identity taught me to doubt myself. if i was not this enough, i was not that enough, either. for a child learning they are neither here nor there, seeds of self-doubt sprout into stems that split in the wind. every gust blows them over and strips them of their fragile leaves. unable to stand, they droop until they know not who or what they are.

i was a brittle-stemmed human seeking the sunlight for much of my life.

to be desi-ish is to know that chai is sacred.
if you decline chai, you might not be desi at all.

Why chai why

chai
i'm exhausted
chai pilo
my heart aches
chai piyo
i'm feeling so moody, yaar
chalo, chai piyen
i'm lonely

drink your chai
why?

joy, celebration, or festivity
sorrow, grief, or mourning
it is chai time.

we desi folks
do not speak openly of our emotions
we rarely are real about our feelings
mental illness is taboo.

so what do we do?
chai
we sip so much chai.

chai is the cure-all for the
ailing heart and soul.
our perpetual
pyar ki pyaas
chai ki chyaas
is a bottomless thirst
insatiable

with each cup of chai we
swallow our feelings
yearning for healing.

why?
who needs therapy?
boil your milk and tea leaves
stir stir stir in the secret masala
sweeten
boil and boil and boil
strain out the stresses and worries
sit sip exhale

repeat
why chai
chai is the hope for healing
chai is the mysterious cure
for all the angst
that will not be
spoken or expressed.

chai on repeat.
why chai?
don't ask

just sip sip sip.
do not ask why
you still feel empty.

there is fleeting chai-n चैन
in chai.

maybe we chant
chai-n
lips whispering prayer
as we sip.

to be desi-ish is to decline the mithai—what heresy.
do we all relish our sweets?

Death by gulaab jamun

let me tell you a horror story
of an aunty
who was allergic
to dairy
gluten
nuts shuts too.
hay haye
thoo thoo
who's ever heard
of such a curse?
what kind of goree cursed
this aunty?
she can't even eat
mithai
or sip chai.
what kind of living hell
is this kala jadoo?
can you imagine
never ever tasting
a paratha dripping with ghee?
no paneer bhajee?
can you imagine saying
"nah thank you"
when the ladoos shadoos
are passed around?
drinking earl grey or darjeeling
or assam with no sugar
and calling it tea?
what curse is this for a desi

to be condemned to death
by gulaab jamun
because she is allergic to
goddess only knows what?

we don't believe in allergies
we would just
say our mantra shantra
eat the damn
gulaab jamun.

to be desi-ish is to simultaneously practice & reject traditions.

Head cover, sir dhak lo

i confess i loathed the elders' reminders to
cover my head.

i used to wonder about the aunties
stirring daal with their chunnis
wrapped around their heads.
i would judge them harshly
for their old-timey ways.

liberate yourselves!
shed your head coverage.
shed the patriarchal bondage.

we don't need to cover ourselves.
we can be free.

let go of the veils and dupattas!
let go of the old ways,
i found myself thinking.

you wouldn't find me anywhere with
a scarf on my head or
a shawl over my shoulders.

i needed to feel free
even with kin and community,
as an educated person rarely conforming to tradition,
i could not appear other.[6]

imagine my surprise to
find that these days,
i've been head covering
without consciously realizing it,

like our ancestral women,
wearing dupattas of ivory or saffron or gold.

these head coverings
bring me safety, comfort, and solace.

it's as if our ancestral spirits
have removed a veil from my heart
whispered a
truth to my soul.
true freedom comes

not from giving up our traditions
but from embracing our own authentic ways.

sir dhak lo.
cover your head.

to be desi-ish
and head cover selectively
like the bibis in punjab
is to revoke the number imperial feminism does on me.

Identified by our cultural practices

We are identified by our adornings
ਸਲਵਾਰ ਕਮੀਜ਼ ਦੁਪੱਟਾ ਚੁੰਨੀ

We are identified by
ਸਾਡਾ ਮੰਤਰ ਅਤੇ ਬੋਲੀ

We are identified by our movements.

We are identified by our feasts—dawat,
chai & gulaab jamun,
samosa, parothe, kebab, biryani, & tarka daal.
Most of all, we are identified by our unspoken meanings &
subtle gestures, head nods & inflections,
only discernible
to those who share our ways, too.

---

6. Chandra Mohanty, "Under Western Eyes: Feminist Scholarship and Colonial Discourses," Feminist Review 30, no. 1 (1988): 61-88, doi.org/10.1057/fr.1988.42.

Elusive authenticity

a friend once remarked after tasting my daal, infused with cumin and turmeric and stewed in tomato broth, that it was not authentic. she offered me a recipe and her *corrections*.
i declined.

to be desi-ish is to admire your kin & yearn to be more desi.
to be desi-ish is to understand that pressure is often confused for love.

to be desi-ish is to be a dutiful daughter, only thirteen and already burdened with expectations around marriage.

She

my she/her/hers are pronounced in
desi life as an endless
list of rules,
regulations,
and requirements.

Lessons in obedience

we memorized our lessons.

we learned by rote memorization. we recited our knowledge word for word from the textbooks sent from india to the high commission in tanzania. we learned sanskrit and sang the anthem of a faraway land. we wore uniforms and we marched in straight lines. we sat in neat rows. we kept our silence. we raised our hands. we did not speak out

of turn. we spoke when we were spoken to. we did not speak out of
turn. we obeyed. we followed the rules. we deferred to our teachers.
we were commanded to respect our elders.

we memorized our lessons. we memorized obedience.

A note to my aunties from my younger self

dear desi aunties and mamis,
real talk. sach bolo.
you are raising your children on a steady diet of
toxic masculinity and patriarchal abuse.

what is all this rishta obsession?
what if you didn't force your daughters to marry?
what if you didn't tell your twelve-year-olds that marriage
defines their purpose?

what if you stopped matchmaking?
what if you stopped all this shaadi marriage frenzy?

you say you do this because you love us.

love isn't control.
love isn't authority.
love isn't fearful.
love doesn't shame.
love doesn't threaten or require obedience.

you control and patronize us in the name of love.

let us call it what it is: this is abuse.
what if you let your daughter just be?

let us daughters breathe?
let us find our own way?
let us love and be loved how we choose?

let me ask you:
how has marriage suited you?
how was your rishta?
were you shackled into servitude?
while secretly wishing for your paintbrushes or sitar?

did you find your joy?
did you hide your poetry, stop reading for pleasure, and forget your profession?
were you secretly seething, abused by the in-laws?
did the uncles' moods rule every day?

did you cry silent suffering into your pillow many a night?
did you consider ending your life or running away to free yourself?
damn the married life, and fantasize about your escape?

did you succumb and become numb to the abuse and think this was "normal"?

abuse is not normal is not love.
love does not control.
love does not shame.
love does not demand obedience.
love does not justify silence.

and here you are, repeating the cycles of abuse with your children.

you dare arrange their rishtas, fates, and futures
to set them up
for exploitation and abuse?

why not set those daughters free of
expectations
constrictions
control
fear
shame?

why not raise them to
create
build
imagine
their own life and love
with or without
marriage?

> ***to be desi-ish is***
> ***to live under***
> ***patriarchal cultural norms***
> ***even as i rage defiantly***
> ***within.***

Who taught me to love hate myself?

the patriarchy taught me to hate myself. compulsory heterosexist marriage obsession is hateful. we are taught that, born female, we have no value or worth outside of patriarchal parameters.

colorism taught me lies about myself. classism taught me i was labor.

under the guise of good intentions, aunties and strict teachers who uttered words of colorism, casteism, and classism put me in my place. i came to doubt my worth. i learned early in life that the world does not value little brown girls with modest financial means residing on african soil.

i was fourteen when an elder
informed me that i was not to marry a Black person even
though i lived in africa.
we are indians and indians marry their own kind.

Disgraceful desi

what could a desi daughter possibly do to be condemned a disgrace?

he was Black.
he had been married before.
he was muslim.
he had a ten-year-old son.

log kya kahenge? what will society say?
this tight rope that binds desi daughters to tradition.

i transgressed.
i defied.

i became a disgrace
by marrying my beloved.

log are still talking about it.
it has been twenty years and counting since i
became a disgraceful desi daughter.

my desi-ish ways are disruptive and have had me reprimanded. i am called a "disgraceful desi." like the *feminist killjoy*, the disgraceful desi might reclaim her title to turn the injury into an honor.[7]

---

7. Sara Ahmed, *The Feminist Killjoy Handbook: The Radical Potential of Getting in the Way* (Penguin, 2024).

*to be desi-ish is to be both
constrained and privileged by model minority myths.
it is to be both the oppressed and the oppressor.*

What desi anti-Blackness looks like

Audre Lorde cautioned, "For the master's tools will never dismantle the master's house. They may allow us temporarily to beat him at his own game, but they will never enable us to bring about genuine change."[8]

when we are neither
Black nor
white
when we are benefitting from
proximity
to whiteness
or when we fleetingly
feign allegiance with other folks of color

when we are discreetly
anti-Black while
claiming to be a "people of color"

but maybe we feel shame about being oppressed
so we ally with whiteness

we shy away from our Black kin
ignoring our collective humanity

we minimize their pain
while claiming to be discriminated against
all the while choosing
to drown in whiteness

---

8. Audre Lorde, "The Master's Tools Will Never Dismantle the Master's House," in *Sister Outsider: Essays and Speeches* (Crossing Press, 2007), 110.

denying our pigmentation
justifying gentrification

we who are overly invested
in being the exceptions
we seek to shine as "model minorities"
we are messengers of the master's rules
claiming we all must pull ourselves up by our
boot
straps

but we are the master's fools
with our boots on the throats of
our Black kin
to climb up the master's ladder
and in climbing claim
that our brethren's lives don't matter

we are complicit in adding insult injury and harm

we the brown
the neither here
nor there

we the brown
we must shift this tide
instead of drowning ourselves in whiteness
to obfuscate our pigmentation

we could turn the tide
we could step off the throats of Black folks
and kneel bend tend with
deep bows of our backs

not to the masters as their fools
but in solidarity with Black folks

knowing and living the truth
that any gain we claim
at their expense
is only pain

pain pain pain
we all fall
we all drown
could we just know this without a doubt

no lives nor gains nor climbs matter
unless and until Black lives matter.

> *to be desi-ish is to edit, to correct ourselves when we write capital "D" desi and lowercase "b" Black.*

Punjabi beti | बेटी

i am the first-born beti
to a first-born beta
first granddaughter poti
in a family of punjabi
refugees torn apart
by partition.

लोग and दुनिया | ਲੋਕ and ਦੁਨੀਆ

punjab existed before india.
punjab existed before pakistan.
punjab existed before the raj.
punjab is the land of my ancestors.

Root truth

the more i water the roots of my heritage, the more i grow into myself.

when i claim my roots and adore my multidimensional heritage i grow wings.

to be desi-ish is to identify as Punjabi but not as Indian. Much to my chagrin, many of us are mistaught to confuse heritage with nationality.

Identified by imperialism and colonialism

those of us with roots in the south asian continent
were colonial subjects. imperialism and colonialism
are processes of occupation and domination. colonial
forces took over, ruled, and partitioned the lands of
my ancestors. imperial forces continue to suppress
our heritage and dominate our ideas,
behaviors, minds, bodies, and spirits. when we speak of
desi-ish postcolonial identity and heritage, colonialism
and imperialism must be named and confronted as
defining realities. we speak of both in past tense, but
they are omnipresent.

to be desi-ish is to often be unaware of one's true history and ancestry.

No watan

I am a descendant of those who were
permanently & as yet irrevocably made refugees,
removed from their
homelands when Punjab,
the land of five rivers,
was partitioned by colonial
forces under the guise of national
independence.

There is no right of return.[9]
There is no watan.
What is the destiny of multifaith
Punjabis who became refugees
during partition?
It is perpetual landlessness bereft of
belonging.

to be desi-ish is to interrogate the colonial histories resulting in the current border regimes throughout south asia.

---

9. Here, I use the term "right of return" to place Partition and the occupation of Palestine in conversation. Many displaced and stateless people struggle for this human right, and the term "right of return" is commonly associated with the struggle of Palestinians who were displaced during the Nakba to return home.

Partition—we are kin

on the 14th of august 1947, pakistan was born.
on the 15th of august 1947, india was "independent."
the british called it transfer of power.
the indians called it independence day.

it was partition day.[10]
one and a half million
lives were lost.

among them, my maternal grandmother.
1% of the world's people became refugees.

my ancestors were uprooted from their punjab and fled across a
random border to the other side. they left everything.
partition.

they never went back.
none of us have ever returned.
we carry the traumas of uprooting as soul wounds. passed
down generation to generation.
we bear the soul scars of severance from homelands.
partition.

we are in parts, separated from each other. we do
not recall that we are the same people.
we the pakistani, we the hindustani, we the bangladeshi. we the
muslim, we the sikh, we the hindu.

we are kin.

---

10. Independence days might mislead us into thinking that there is a "post" to colonialism. This reframe signals that days celebrating the making of borders and partitions are ongoing colonial violence.

we do not remember.

78+ years.

i remember. are
we free yet?

> *to be desi-ish means*
> *to not hold any national pride in india*
> *but rather claim sovereignty for kashmir*
> *as i declare kinship with pakistan.*

घबराहट | Ghabrahat

this is the word in my mother's tongue
that signifies anxiety intermixed with paralyzing fear.
when i write what i write
about desi islamophobia,
my desi kin
are struck with paralyzing fear.
they try to silence me.

my words, they fear,
will have me attacked, exiled, or worse.
they fear for my safety,
that my words calling out hindu
supremacy and fascism will be the
end of me.

                              ghabrahat.

their fears are not far-fetched.
their ghabrahat is not imagined.
read the news coming out of india.
patriarchal hindutva supremacy is ruling.

there are no words adequate to convey that ghabrahat.

                we cannot chup karo
                or else that will be the end.

i am desi-ish
because when i recently traveled to the desh, i
was required to apply for a visa.
claiming kin in pakistan would have had this visa entry
declined.
i left out a few details.

Gayatri Sethi

i am desi-ish because i question
the distrusts & dissensions among
south asians.

we are at war with our kin.
partition is now.

we speak of 1947 as if it were the past
but partition rages on in us and around us.

it festers in the rampant islamophobia among hindus.
islamophobia is a disease my kin contracted in partition.

we carry and pass on the traumas of uprooting as soul wounds of hate
planted and exploited in us by colonizers,
passed down generation to generation.

we bear the soul scars of severance from truth.

in beforetimes, muslims and hindus and sikhs were bound in oneness.

partition is not over.

we still wage war with ourselves.

to be a desi-ish punjabi grandchild of partition is to
carry intergenerational transferred trauma.

i have heard it said that unless trauma is transformed, it
is transferred.
this truth resonates tragically within me.[11]

---

11. Tabitha Mpamira-Kaguri, "Trauma Not Transformed Is Trauma Transferred," hosted by TedxOakland, public lecture, November 2019, posted December 3, 2019 by Tedx Talks, YouTube, https://www.youtube.com/watch?v=b4loBphYCXI.

Seeing red for kashmir

> I cannot drink water
> It is mingled with the blood of young men who have died up in the mountains.
> I cannot look at the sky
> It is no longer blue; but painted red.
> —Kashmiri poet[12]

i'm seeing red for kashmir.
our tricolor flags are waving in
shades of red.

why are we not mourning?

after 78 years of partition,
the flag-waving patriots
are warmongering, bloodthirsty,
proclaiming hindu supremacy.

india, the democracy, is no more.
was it ever.
we, the colonized, became colonizers.

have we counted the dead?
do we see red?
do we bleed red?

i do not go to temple,
but i surely pray
we will be healed from ingesting this poison
of toxic patriarchy and fiery patriotism
that boil together to make us fascist occupiers
who wave flags to display
our own freedoms
even as we defile and destroy

---

12. Muzamil Jaleel, "Poetry in commotion," The Guardian, July 29, 2002, www.theguardian.com/world/2002/jul/29/kashmir.india.

the freedoms of our kin.
i'm seeing red for kashmir.
i'm seeing red for india.

the democracy is a farce
we are now occupiers
we, the colonized, became colonizers.

let us wave the red-stained flag at half-mast.

i saw red for kashmir long before i was told by relatives that we have ancestry in this land.
i am rarely surprised when i learn facts
that confirm my feelings.

i remind myself that life is a sort of remembering.

i am named gayatri.
i am the one who knows
without knowing.

आज़ादी | آزادی

Fascist state

The indian state commits pogroms against sikhs & muslims while occupying kashmir.

What happens when our cultural heritage is circumscribed by a fascist state that denies our sovereignty?

We choose to be Punjabi or Kashmiri,
but are disloyal to indian nationalism & fascism.

Filling in blanks

i am ever relearning histories
mistaught to me by colonial design
in textbooks fraught with blanks.
I was never taught to seek ancestral knowledge
about what it means to be descended
from punjabi sikh or kashmiri lineages.
every time i stumble on missing histories,
unfilled blanks,
or misinformation,
i recall how much of what i learned
from relatives & schools alike
is cultural programming,
propaganda,
missing histories—incomplete—
awaiting us to fill in the blanks—
circumscribed by the indian fascist state.

to be desi-ish
is to hold privileges while being intimate with
oppression.

What if we unbelong?

what happens at the intersections of faith

class

caste

when we enjoy privilege
of one kind while being
oppressed by our own kind?

what are distinctly desi words for caste?
Jati & codes Savarna.
Sanghhi. Bhakt.
... some of them sound like slurs & may remain unsaid.

Meditations on lateral violence[13]

lateral violence happens when we desi folks identity
police each other.
when we turn on each other to
protect power or whiteness.
when we internalize
the misleading narratives about us.
when one of us
is made to feel like they are not one of us.

when desi-ness
is weaponized by those who presume to be
the keepers of all that is desi.

desi-ish? there is no such thing.
you are a fraud.
who do you think you are?
what's your aukat?

---

13. Australian Human Rights Comission, "Lateral violence in Aboriginal and Torres Strait Islander communities," in Social Justice Report 2011, December 2012.

to be desi-ish is to be mis-casted regularly by those invested in casteism while denying its prevalence.

lateral violence happens so often in desi circles and communities that i have come to expect it as the norm. diasporic folks like me who have no other word or term to identify ourselves, with roots in south asia but no fixed ties to the subcontinent, are the targets of considerable lateral violence. identity wounds are inflicted.

we are misnamed by our own communities. we are disowned in words and deeds. we are cut off from our roots by those who claim to have ownership of them. we are often told by our very own relatives that we have no right to the desh. we are reprimanded for being inauthentic. if we ever speak honestly about our heritage or utter words of caution about toxic cultural traits, we are shamed.

those of us who are also mixed or blended in our caste and faith identifications, as i am, are often subject to identity exile.[14]

it is not unusual for well-educated and aware folks to misidentify my caste or misuse my identifications. they presume i am hindu. i am not. they do not consider how my baháí faith interacts in complex ways with my family's caste of origin. bahujan. identifications are fluid and nuanced within the vastness of what being desi means. most of us do not remember all this as we constrain and confine each other by performing lateral violence in the form of identity policing.

any wonder as a younger person, i distanced myself from my desi roots. this distancing is a form of self-harm. as i age, i have come to see self-naming as a reclamation of my cultural heritage.

how do fractured identities like mine evolve and grow?

**to be desi-ish is
to realize
that wherever desis reside,
casteism prevails.**

Gayatri Sethi

to be desi-ish is to practice unbelonging by refusing to conform to cultural silencing.

Chup kar | चुप कर

dear culturally maladjusted disrupters who've been silenced by society, family, and community—
keep on speaking.

keep on raising the issues.

i'm the desi annoying and embarrassing her people by talking openly about all the taboo topics.

queerness: i will discuss it.
islamophobia: i will reject it.
mental illness: i will not ignore it.
anti-Blackness: i will dismantle it.
abuse: i will call it out.
casteism: i will not stand for it.
sikhphobia: i stand by my kin.

i found my voice, and i will use it.

Disconnection is lifelessness.
Silence breeds purposelessness in me.
I was not born, I do not live, I was not raised for silence.

chup kar.
this is the deep desi cultural conditioning that is locked in me.
it blocks me.

---

14. Identity exile is a term I use to refer to those who by choice or not are exiled from their own identifications. For instance, those who are not considered desi but due to multicultural identifications become desi-ish. I wonder if exile from identity is like exile from lands.

still, i will not look the other way.

log kya kahenge? i could care less what people think or say.
i refuse to align with the silencing chup kar ways of my people.

these toxic cultures of shame and silencing breed abuse.

i aim to be a cycle breaker.

Boli | ਬੋਲੀ

our poetry is spoken word.
you hear us not.
we write here.
you see us not.
we right here.
you feel us not.
boliyaan.
our spoken word is spoken word.

In order to shift from "i" to we, i am learning to inquire:

Are there reasons beyond me as an individual that might explain my unbelonging to desi-ness?

We might situate conversations about desi identities within imperial historical contexts and systems of oppression like casteism, patriarchy, anti-Blackness, and so on.

Where do desi cultural malpractices originate?

to be desi-ish is to understand that being in diaspora means that we are disconnected by colonial intent & that belonging is elusive by design.

Desi-ish diaspora

Multitudes of us all over the globe are desi-ish diaspora peoples.

We were transplanted,
by empire—British, French & Dutch,
displaced, relocated, indentured

throughout time,
disconnected from the subcontinent
to relive in distinctly desi ways throughout
places known as
Fiji, Guyana, Trinidad, Suriname, South Africa, East Africa,
& beyond.

We were jahaji, girmitiya,
indo-Caribbeans, indo-Africans, Hindoestanen,
indo-laborers of empire toiling on plantation soil,
tilling, plowing, raising,
sugar, cotton & tea,
not enslaved, but not free.

Desi diaspora struggles, labors, divisions,
disconnections by empire's designs
are distinctly diasporic.
For these diasporic folks,
There is no return,
not knowing where they originate.

There is healing in learning new words & concepts
to name our disconnected & connected histories & presents.
Remembering is a key to connecting,
so how do we unlock desi diaspora connections?

Bakwaas or pyar | बकवास or प्यार

to call out the bakwaas
in our cultural or discursive norms
results in being shunned and disowned.
we know that the moment
we utter even a mutter
of complaint or critique
of the ways in which
desi patriarchy colorism
aukaat oppressions
are abusive and harmful

we risk our belonging.
we must make brave choices:
chup kar and stay safely belonging
or speak out and risk unbelonging.

i made my choices.
no bakwaas
only radical revolutionary pyar
for self, sach, and haqq. सच | حق

Gayatri Sethi

Notes

Reflection Invitation:

What are your working definitions of and connections between the following terms or concepts?

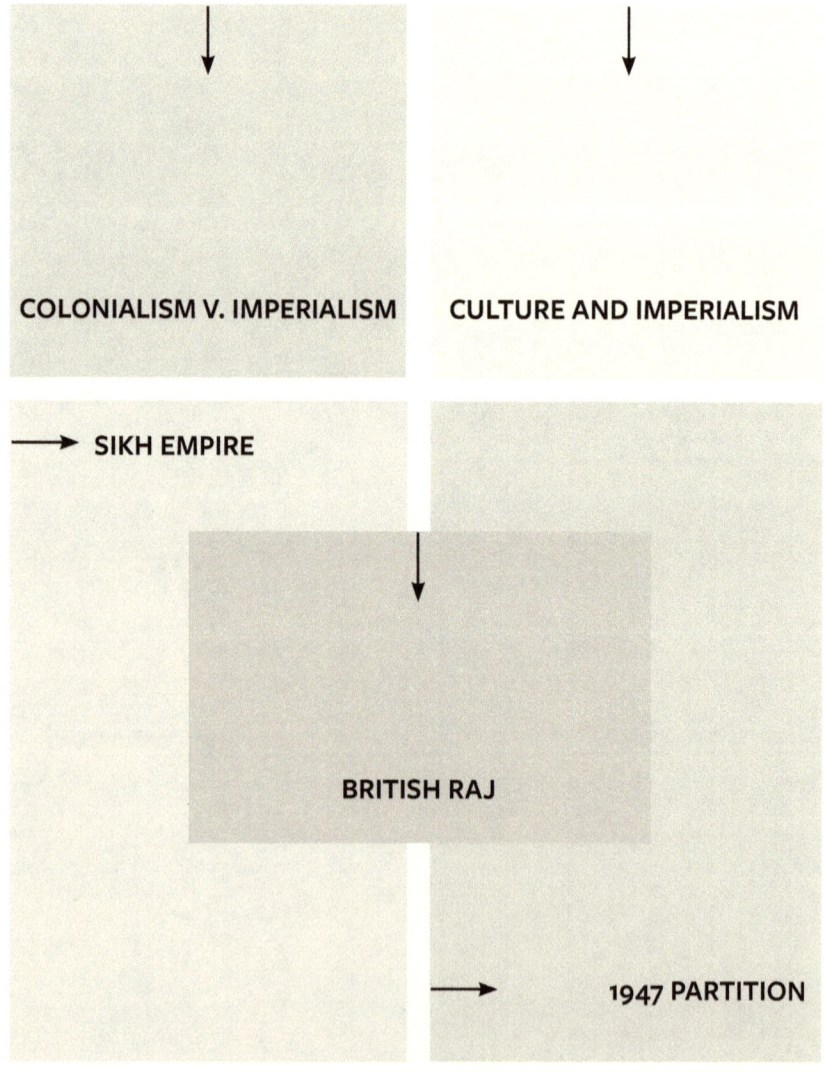

COLONIALISM V. IMPERIALISM

CULTURE AND IMPERIALISM

SIKH EMPIRE

BRITISH RAJ

1947 PARTITION

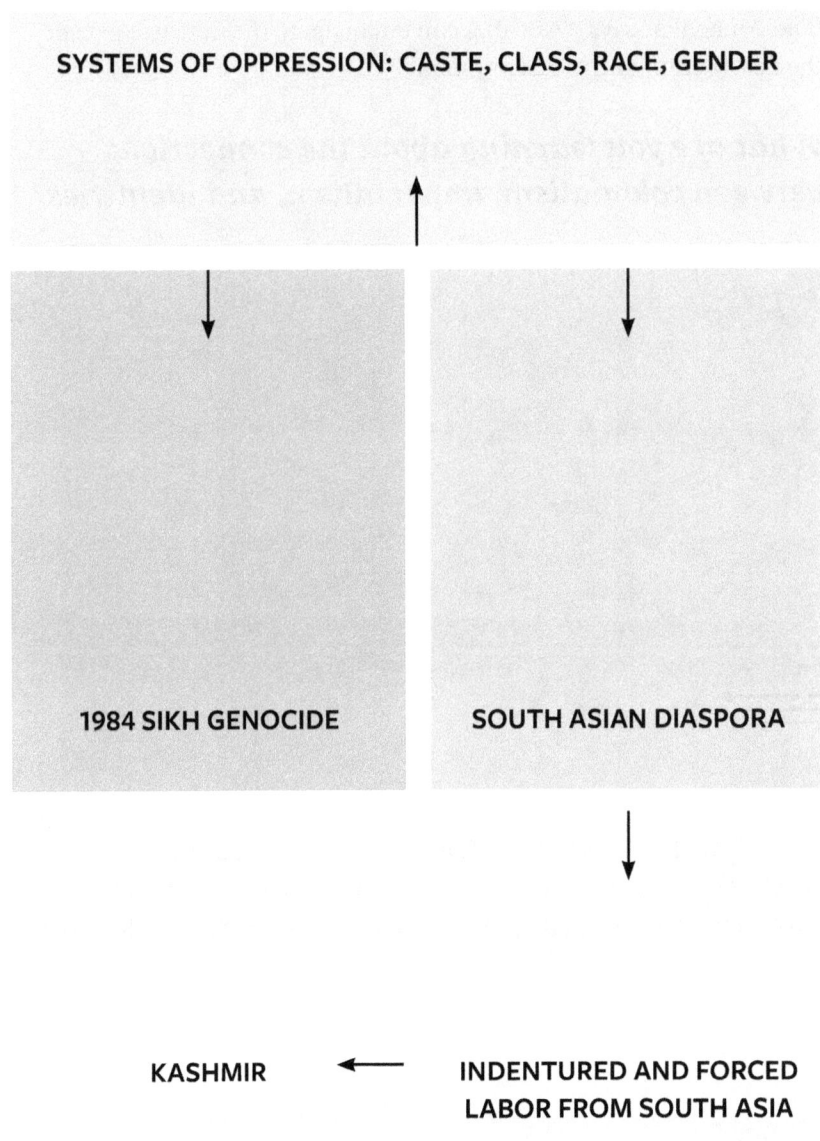

Inquiries

What are you unlearning about South Asian identities?

B. R. Ambedkar says, "Nothing can emancipate the outcaste except the destruction of the caste system."[15]

What are you learning about the connections between colonialism, imperialism, and identities?

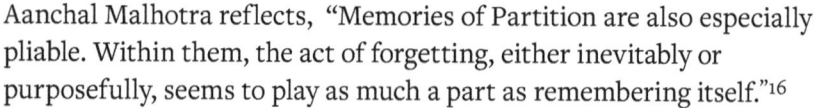

Aanchal Malhotra reflects, "Memories of Partition are also especially pliable. Within them, the act of forgetting, either inevitably or purposefully, seems to play as much a part as remembering itself."[16]

What are you relearning about identity and belonging?

---

15. B. R. Ambedkar, *Annihilation of Caste: The Annotated Critical Edition*, ed. S. Anand (Verso, 2014), 18.

16. Aanchal Malhotra, "Partition of India: Objects that tell the story of a mass exodus," CNN Style, August 8, 2017, https://www.cnn.com/style/article/india-pakistan-partition-remnants-of-separation/index.html.

AFRICAN·ISH

Where are you from?

Any attempts to respond to this inquiry would lead me to Africa.
i am identified by African-ish geographies.
By birth, i am placed on the African continent in Shinyanga, Tanzania.
By nationality & passport, i am a citizen of Botswana.

> *to be African-ish is to perpetually offer history & geography lessons when asked where you are from.*

Indo-Africans

For hundreds of years, brown folks from the South Asian subcontinent have lived, thrived, and sometimes been exiled from Africa.

These peoples were referred to as Indo-Africans but not Afro-Indians.

No thanks to colonialism, Indians of various castes and faiths were forcibly brought to parts of Africa and the Caribbean from the 1860s onwards.

This complex Asian diaspora in Africa history deserves further study. Though I am implicated in this history, my family is among more recent immigrants to Africa.

To be African-ish is to understand ways we identify to connect
us to land & people:
Who are your people?
Where is your home village?
Where are your lands?

Am I Motswana?[17]

To be Motswana is to be in a relationship to land that
immigrants and settlers do not hold.

Heart home

if anyone were ever to ask me
where i aspire
to call home,
where i yearn to return,
where my heart feels warm,
where my mind wanders often,
where my soul knows calm,
without skipping a heartbeat,
i would say:
anywhere i was raised
in Africa!

to be African-ish is to remember the distinction between
citizens and naturalized citizens.

---

17. Many debates proliferate about who is a settler and whether immigrants or descendants of indentured folks can be setters, too. Settlerism is characterized by extractive relationships to Indigenous lands that many people replicate.

Citizen?

Election Day in Botswana.
I am 53 years old. I have never voted.
I was born in Tanzania, a country that did not validate my citizenship.
For much of my life, I carried the passport of my Indian family's background,
but not my belonging by birth.
When I was a college student, my family became citizens of Botswana, where we resided and considered our "forever home."
I was living as a student with an F-1 visa in america then.
I reside in the united states now.
My status here is complicated at best.
I came here as an F-1.
Then, I became an H-1B. Authorized to be employed. Legal.
After I married an american, it took me many years to get a "green card."
I have not seriously considered becoming a citizen.
I take pride in my Botswana passport.
Becoming a voting american was neither my aim nor aspiration.
But on election day, I wish I could vote in my naturalized home country alongside my Batswana kin for democracy's sake.
I could never vote in Tanzania, the land of my birth.
I've never voted in India (or Pakistan for that matter), the lands of my ancestry.
I've never been in Botswana during an election cycle.
I wish I could be teleported to an election booth.

In america, I do not have the right to vote.
Maybe I never will?

Even though I shun flag-waving patriotism,
I wish I could vote.
Perhaps, if only once, to feel like a citizen of somewhere.
Until we build another world and another system,
I trust that though the vote is not a revolution, it matters.

Although many of us are entangled in citizenship and passports as markers of national identity, we ought to inquire further. Is citizenship a colonial construct rooted in border imperialism?

African-ish Geographies

Geographies change over time and with politics.

The origin story of today's African geography is colonial even though the history of Africa neither begins nor ends with colonialism.

What was decided about Africa at the Berlin Conference in 1885? Did any Africans have a say or attend?

What is the ongoing legacy of Europeans cooperating on how to divide and conquer Africa?

Whose arbitrary borders still carve up Africa into 54 nations even after supposed postcolonial independence?

Do we inquire how or why the vast continent is often treated with singularity?

to be African-ish is to unlearn colonial geographies.

Diasporic exhaustion

Africa is not a country.
Word to the wise
from a person born
and raised on the
continent.

Africa is not a country.
Do not assume its uniformity.
Open your eyes to
its multitudes.

Africa is not a country.
Its multiple realities defy singularity.

Where?

Where are you from?

Gaborone.

Where?

(Breath.)

Botswana.

Where is that?

(Deep breath.)
Neighboring South Africa.

to be African-ish is to encounter lies about the continent perpetuated even by those who claim to be informed.

Debunking African stereotypes

All over the world, misinformation about Africa persists to this day. Wherever I travel, I am forced to defend or shed light on what growing up there is really like. These conversations are steeped in racist myths and "single stories"[18] about Africa.
There are so many widespread lies about Africa (the land, cultures, and peoples) that people hold as common knowledge.

Why must we debunk African stereotypes?
Maybe because most of us hold them.

Dominant narratives and counternarratives

All over Africa, there are sayings that translate as:
The story of the hunt is told by the hunter. Until the story of the hunt is told by the lion, we miss the full story.

Hunter: What are the dominant narratives about African cultures, peoples, and places?
Lion: What are some counternarratives?

to be African-ish is to relearn African history & geography perpetually because we are mistaught so much.

---

18. Chimamanda Ngozi Adichie, "The Danger of a Single Story," TED, 2009, https://www.ted.com/talks/chimamanda_adichie_the_danger_of_a_single_story.

Why I am African-ish

For an indian-descended citizen of Botswana like me to claim to be African-ish is equal parts
+ resistance to Apartheid racial categories
+ commentary on the somewhat ridiculous nature of identity talk
+ dreaming of pan-African racial solidarity.

Maybe i am African-ish because i was born planted in East African soil and grew shoots under the southern African sun. Although i was a brown seedling planted and replanted there, i am also an uprooted desi African.

i wish i were a rooted tree.
i wish to be a majestic baobab overlooking the glorious Zambezi.

In reality, i might be a healing tulsi herb in a clay pot perched precariously on a windowsill. My holy leaves would nourish and soothe ailments. i am certainly not the money plant desis cultivate in our homes for good luck.

> ***to be African-ish is to know where most of your childhood & formative years were lived.***

Gayatri Sethi

Are we identified by our childhood memories?

Playing and praying for belonging

The five-year-old me was straight up confused.

I was a brown African speaking Hindi to my parents who spoke Punjabi to each other in private while we all spoke Kiswahili and English in public.

We prayed interchangeably in English, Hindi, and Farsi.
We learned interchangeably in Kiswahili, Hindi, and English. We played interchangeably in Kiswahili, Hindi, and English. We ate ugali and daal and bhajiya and mandazi and most of all, we relished ananasi sweeter than the sweetest pineapple you ever tasted.

Saturday mornings at the beach nearby where Indian Ocean breezes would lull us softly into relaxed exhales.
Madafu fresh coconut water sipped, we danced and swam in sunny glee.

These flashes of childhood joys, of splashing in carefree abandon, rolling around in beach sand remain with me always.

The eight-year-old me was straight up flexible.
Come Sundays, we began our days chanting in Farsi and Arabic at children's classes and devotions at the Bahá'í Center.

Next, we went, heads and legs covered, hearts reverent, to serve and partake of the langar at the Gurudwara where our chacha spent his days and some nights at the Khalsa club.
Where were our silver wrist adornments proving that we belonged here?
I might have wondered in confused flexible silence.

I might have prayed for a kara ਕੜਾ of my own.

African-ish Histories

Truth & reconciliation history

There are many stories to be told about how many nations, after formal colonial governance ended, resisted the presence of those brought to their lands by the colonizers.

People of Indian/Asian descent were brought to Africa for a specific colonial purpose.
We were master's tools.

If there were truth and reconciliation commissions for us, too, we would need to confess and be accountable for all the ways we brown folks perpetuate harms against the rightful keepers of the lands to which we were brought by colonial powers. This means that we became accustomed to using disciplinary and divisive tactics of the colonial authorities on each other.

We, brown folks, were master's tools.
We were employed to exert power over our Black compatriots.
Whether by force or by stealth, we abuse our Black kin.

Indo-Africans perpetuate harm on African lands.
Have we told this truth and reconciled?

Apartheid history

Apartheid happens where settler colonialism meets segregation meets enslavement.
All three oppressive systems intersected simultaneously to oppress the original keepers of the lands of southern Africa.
I was alive to witness both the deep systemic oppressions of apartheid and the revolutionary resistance movements across the border from Gaborone, only a few kilometers away from South Africa.

Many of my classmates, neighbors, and teachers were South Africans of all hues and views about the apartheid regime. The South African Defense force would often raid our town in the middle of the night in search of folks who were exiles or suspected of being affiliated with the resistance movement.
This terror resurfaces in my nightmares to this day.
This visceral memory guides me when I identify apartheid structures elsewhere in the world.

to be African-ish is to be raced brown while being from a continent raced Black.

Indians Raced by Apartheid

During Apartheid times in South Africa, a racial hierarchy was enforced.[19]

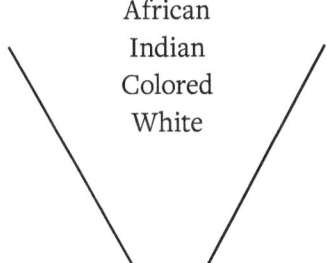

African
Indian
Colored
White

Expat

What does it mean to always be an expatriate and rarely be considered a patriot?

I grew up in Shinyanga, Dar es Salaam, and Gaborone. With the exception of a brief time in Chandigarh with my maternal grandparents as a toddler, I did not know India as a home.
We were expats. We had work permits with expiration dates. I recall

---

19. I deliberately flip this hierarchy to indicate that the majority of the population was oppressed by the minority.

how every two to three years, my parents' worry and uncertainty resurfaced. Would we need to return to Delhi? What would we even do there? None of us remembered how to live or earn a living there. We prayed, hoped, and did our earnest best to be good guests worthy of contract renewals. Pa worked long hours with exemplary dedication. My parents served with the kind of seva ethic that all their faith and cultural practices encouraged. Pa would say, "Work is worship." Ma would reply, "Seva is the only way."

What does being a brown expat mean? It is a precarious life, living caught in the balance, knowing that the advantages we might enjoy are temporary and incomparable to those of the European and american expats. We rarely speak of these inequities as we are supposed to be grateful immigrants.

As a child of Indian expats, I learned that we do not buy furniture. We do not invest resources in material objects that do not fit into suitcases. We do not have heirlooms. We are ready to pack everything we need into two suitcases, twenty kilos each. We know that we are guests here. We are ever uncertain as we are wishful that we could call here, wherever here may be, home.

to be African-ish means that racial hierarchy places me precariously, even on the continent, subject to white dominance.

Wazungu

I was taught to defer to the wazungu.[20]

We pleased the wazungu.
We were not to be cheeky to them. The repercussions could be dire.
We swallowed our pride and dimmed our dignity.
We appeased the wazungu.

Somehow, we held on to our humanity.

How were we taught to defer to whiteness without question?

Internalized colonialism

Subjects like me are objects of colonial intervention. We often consume ideologies, practices, and belief systems that perpetuate harm against ourselves and others. Often, we learn how to be colonial subjects through western style schooling.
Schooling colonizes our minds, bodies, and spirits.

The legacy of colonialism is alive.
Decolonization has many meanings.
It is not an event. To me, it is a holistic process.
It means redressing the damage to our cultures and ideas as much as to our lands and histories.

---

20. Throughout East Africa, foreigners, especially Europeans, are referred to as wazungu. In the singular, muzungu or mzungu means a person who is lost or wandering without aim.

Africans abroad

We live in a world where Africans are expected to go abroad. Our success is often measured by our stints overseas. Whether we go away to seek education or travel regularly as a sign of our wealth, we confuse alignment with Europe or north america as aspirational.

I am an African abroad who is tired of inhabiting a world in which we of the African soil seek to leave. We are made to be oblivious to the histories and presence of colonialism and imperialism. We are taught to cape for whiteness.

When I point out that brown and Black folks who live on the African continent center whiteness because of internalized oppression, I am negated.

I refuse to cape for whiteness in the motherland.
I am tired of the violence done daily to Black and brown bodies globally.

Home-ish

Something about being "home"—the home where my aging mother now resides—that brings me grief:

Even at home I am a misfit.

A blessing about Gaborone life is that I can leave for decades, but when I return, I am still oriented. I know where what is. I understand how things flow here. I hear words and see their meanings. I can make the collective gestures that those not from here will barely notice. I can bump into people I knew as a youth randomly in familiar places. Years go by and we can still recognize each other. It is truly a blessing to have a place like this where we can be visitors and right at home. If I'm not thinking about it, it's as if I've always been here.

> Dumela.

I suppose this is the fleeting sense that many call home. When I am here, I am home-ish.

to be African-ish is to remember that even if home is not a place, it can be placed.

Where we rest in peace

Pa's extended family could not comprehend why he would decline the Hindu last rites of his ancestors. He requested in his will that we lay him to rest in peace in Botswana. He specified that he was not to be cremated.
If he is buried there, isn't this the place I ought to consider my home?

So it is.

> Dumela.

Trauma memory

i am a hyphenated human. i am a punctuated human. i am a human ever chasing my humanity . . .
there is enough childhood trauma and racial trauma and immigrant trauma and interpersonal trauma and relational violence trauma and healthcare discrimination trauma and we-disown-you trauma and fired trauma and unfairly treated trauma and gender based assault trauma and and and trauma for which there are only neurological symptoms and memory lapses that i write myself into healing on these pages with

DIASPORA-ISH

gaping gaps

silences

lapses

that can as yet not be

remembered

recalled

or healed.

I am often asked why I write in these half sentences lacking form and essay-like clarity. I cannot tell you exactly the moment when my body was shocked by blows. I cannot detail to you how the realities of being told that Africa was only for Africans dawned on our family. I cannot recount too many stories of childhood revelry that are not shadowed by family trauma. My parents were refugees who lived with disabilities and they were unable often to put words to the traumas their bodies and minds held.
They came undone. There is no clarity of memory in me to say why I can barely recall my days in Tanzania or India. Trauma memory is suppressed for survival.
I am asked why I write half thoughts. Why are my observations seemingly inconclusive?
I reply that trauma memory is like this. There is much I have yet to name or process or heal.

The forms of communication of translated, hyphenated, and punctuated humans are slippery, flowing, contradictory, evasive, messy.

i am African-ish because i have called multiple places on the continent home.

Longing for belonging

I pined for our previous home.

I longed to return.
My longing to belong
became an omnipresent heart song.

> *We learned that far away from relatives, an African-ish practice is to form new kinship.*

Embrace humanity

Who taught me to embrace humanity?

Me? Simply.
Ubuntu. Botho.

We were taught from an early age that motho ke motho ka batho.
A person is a person among people.

In my Pa's papers after his passing, I found old photographs. One depicts me as an infant, cradled in the arms of a young woman no older than nineteen or twenty.

Dada

I wonder …

I always knew in my heart that I was raised and loved and lullabied and
rocked and sung to by "dada."

I see that I truly was.

I don't know your name but if my Pa were living, he'd tell me all about you and your people.
I knew you were a member of our family.
I imagine you wrapped me in a kanga cloth and tied me to your back while you swept or washed or cleaned.
I know you bathed and dressed me.
The buttons and hooks weren't easy for my mama, paralyzed on her right side, to manage on her own.
You were her extra pair of hands.

Adopted kin

All over the lands where I grew up, people adopted, raised, and lived in kinship arrangements with folks not related to them. My friends lived with their aunts in the city in order to attend school there. My neighbors adopted their distant cousin because his family passed away from an illness we rarely named that ravaged southern Africa in the eighties and nineties. Many acquaintances orphaned by this epidemic were raised by extended community members.

Being African-ish means to value relationships & collectives.

People create kinship

Sometimes, those who resided in one family home were bound to each other in relations of servitude. While anti-Blackness often inhibited Indo-Africans from claiming kinship, the grace of folks who abided by ubuntu community care ethics adopted me and my family into their own.

Chosen family

Stories of the kinship bonds between people of different races all over the African continent are rarely told. While it is true that racial hierarchies exist and persist, it is also true that people are adopted into chosen family structures. My father's closest friend, Barnabas, was a refugee from Sudan residing in Dar es Salaam. He referred to my pa as "my brother." He bestowed our family with a special place in his family's rituals. Steadfastly, even now, my mother would tie or mail a rakhee for him. We were bonded. I would grow up to do the same for my adopted older brother, who I affectionately call Abuti. I send him a sacred thread each year.
In Botswana, one of my father's students invited him home to visit her family. Her elders declared that my father was "one of them." They walked to a corner of their family compound and gifted it along with two goats to my pa. Pa understood that this privilege came with responsibility. He honored it by visiting the elders, sending funds, and showing up to family gatherings and consultations. These elders gave us each names and mine is Nkai.

When I married, this aunty performed the Tswana wedding duties of a rakgadi for me. My own buas from Delhi did not attend.

Refugees & exiles

I was raised among Iranian refugees. They fled faith-based persecution. They lost their loved ones, property, and rights and resigned themselves to never going home. From an early age, I understood what it means to never be able to return to where you came from.

Among exiles, I learned to hide being Bahá'í. We did not mention certain identities unless we were explicitly asked. Identities could have you permanently displaced and perpetually homeless.

Among refugees, as a descendant of refugees, I learned that the permanence of home is denied to many of us.

When I do talk about identities now, floodgates of inquiry or misunderstanding open wide.

Caregiving

I was raised to be a caregiver.

An invisible truth few people know about me is that I am an able-bodied, first-born female child to two people with disabilities. In days when the term was not in question, they referred to themselves as handicapped.

Western therapists misdiagnosed several conditions, including PTSD. They told me that I grapple with "survivor's guilt" as an adult because I have parents whose lives are informed and constrained by disability.

In my youth, I struggled with shame because our family was so very differently abled.
I resented having limitations and constraints that many of my peers did not. I pretended that disability did not matter.

When I grew up to develop (sometimes invisible) disabilities, I refused to accept them. When I reluctantly did, new learning opened.

As an adult who studies western psychology, I learned that our extended family suffered from intergenerational trauma, addiction, and mental illness. It was denied in hushed tones, desi shame.

Disability within our family is profoundly complex, as it might explain why my father left his home to find a new one.

This is a remembrance:
My Pa referred to himself as handicapped or disabled. He always claimed this identity unapologetically. For much of his life, he was an officer for the Botswana Society of People with Disabilities (BOSPED). All over Botswana, people recognize him as an engaged, disabled citizen to this day. We would go places where he would take space or inform folks who didn't yield to his needs that he was among the bogole, the Setswana word for disabled people.
To the embarrassment of his children, he would drive up to a parking lot and insist on parking near the entrance even if there were no designated parking spots for him. The parking attendants all over town would recognize his vehicle and wave him to his spot. He was blunt, direct, and shunned euphemisms when people mistreated him on account of his disability. I would cringe at these words and actions, and maybe despite knowing better, I still do.
He asked for help and sometimes demanded it from close folks and strangers alike. He used to say, "I'm disabled. I have to ask for help. How else will I survive?" He understood interdependence and so did those around him.

I often look back and wonder how much our staying in Botswana all these years is connected to the culture of caregiving practiced there. The tenderness with which elders and folks like my parents are cared for even by those we don't know by name is not easy to fully explain. What westerners call mutual aid is a normalized way of life elsewhere.

Scars of love

It's time we talk about our scars and let the world see them. I have many scars.
I have a gash above my right eyebrow, well-hidden by my hair pulled over my forehead, just so.
Makeup dabbed and covered, just so.

Recess. Running. Chasing. Running. Bam.
Slam.
Sharp edge of the building.

The chasers stopped cold.
School uniform bleached white drenched redder than red. I don't recall if I cried. I don't remember the pain.

I do remember my nervous mother was the only driver.
She, accompanied by the strict principal, drove me trembling trembling shaking shaking, wavering but brave to the Agha Khan Hospital.

Because love.

Dar es Salaam circa 1979.
Stitched up.
They said the gash was deep and needed double stitches. They said I could've lost my right eye.
The doctor instructed my vegetarian mother to feed me chicken soup because I was so weak and had lost so much blood.
This vegetarian mama went searching for chicken soup and tried to feed it to me.
Because love.

I denied the chicken soup.
Because I'm like that and always have been. I healed.
I could see again. Scarred.
Cautious at recess, but I ran and chased and played again.

It's time we talk about our scars and let the world see them. These scars hold stories of love and fear and healing and love.

Silence as a love language

There are some intimate truths about my life that cannot as yet be spoken even by someone outspoken. These truths will be tucked away because even as I urge myself and others to speak up and speak out, I am keenly aware of the contradictory insight I offer:
Silence, when observed with intention, can be a radical love language, too.

A diamond in name

My Swahili name is Almasi.
I was born in a diamond mining town, Shinyanga, Tanzania.
We moved to Gaborone, Botswana.
Diamonds are the single major source of our wealth.
Batswana take tremendous pride in our diamonds.
We chuckle when we tell the story of how the British left our land in 1966 only months before diamonds were discovered in the depths of our soil.
When strangers quiz me about African droughts and poverty I eye them quizzically and warn them of the dangers of a single story.
Africa is diamond rich.

Global dualities

Core	**Periphery**
First World	**Third World**
West	**Rest**
Global North	**Global South**
Developed	**Underdeveloped**

Where is Africa misplaced in these geopolitics of duality & hierarchy of empire?
Africa is misplaced in not-so-post-colonial empire.
Is it true that Africa is the third within the third world, the periphery of the periphery & the most under of the underdeveloped?
If so, why is it the richest in resources & yet the most extracted impoverished of the Global South?

Walter Rodney tells us, "The true explanation lies in seeking out the relationship between Africa and certain developed countries and in recognizing that it is a relationship of exploitation."[21]

Postcolonialism is a lie

There is no post to
colonialism.
Don't believe me?

to be African-ish is to interrogate dominant narratives & labels that misinform us.

to be African-ish is to comprehend that anti-Blackness is not merely interpersonal;
it is global.

to be African-ish is to be overeducated by colonial schooling, but miseducated in cultural knowledge.

---

21. Walter Rodney, *How Europe Underdeveloped Africa*, (Verso, 2018), 37.

Postcolonial Africa is a neocolonial Africa, too.

We were taught by whiteness culture and whiteness curricula and people of whiteness. Many of my teachers were white South Africans who both condemned Apartheid and were shaped by it. Growing up in the shadow of Apartheid and raised in desi communities, I came to know caste and racial hierarchies intimately. Even if I did not have the words to convey my lived experiences of racism and casteism in sociological terms, I understood what they looked and felt like.

to be African-ish is to side-eye anyone observing independence days even as IMF & UN agencies rule the continent.

Schooled in saviorism

To be raised on African soil is to intimately know that a form of global white supremacy lurks everywhere in the continent.
International development agencies
church groups
global fundraisers
experts
descend upon African and Asian soil,
seeking to save "underdeveloped nations" from
our own presumed backwardness, while defiling our lands with their misinformed prescriptions.
This is the way of the saviorism that is so often rooted in us insidiously.
Permanent damage under the guise of good intentions.
We, the saved, become saviors.
I strive to unlearn the forms of saviorism I inadvertently adopted when I was schooled in the West.

to be African-ish is to be subjects of saviorism. We question if imperialism fronts as saviorism.

Africa-Asia relations

Over two million Chinese people live in Africa now. No exact numbers are available. No accounts about Africa would be complete without adding that Africa today is in an imperial relationship with China. A whitewashed version of African history overlooks the Chinese presence on the continent prior to European arrivals & colonizations.
China is Africa's largest trading partner. What does it mean that currently, most African nations rely on Chinese labor & resources for infrastructure building? Is it a partnership or is it a new empire? Historically, the British & French built roads & railways, so called infrastructure, not for "advancement," but surely for nefarious extraction.
Though the names & faces, styles & times of these imperial forces have changed, Asia-Africa relations are much the same as Europe-Africa relations.
Is any empire gregarious in its relations?

Postcolonial revolutions

Youth and folks of all ages take to the streets in protest
from Niger to Kenya.
As genocides or proxy wars rage from Congo to Sudan to Tigray,
it is abundantly evident that oppressive regimes &
imperial forces of centuries
of extraction persist on African lands.
We may be "independent" from direct colonial rule,
but we are not postcolonial.
Africa knows unfathomable extraction
of resources for centuries.
Africa knows the ongoing extraction of labor & humanity.
Africa cautions the whole world:
anti-Blackness is a genocidal politic.

Is Africa postcolonial?
Ask the descendants of the enslaved.
Ask our kin in Haiti & all over the Caribbean,
but especially ask the African diaspora subjects of empire residing in
empire's core, if they are free of colonialism yet.
Is Africa postcolonial?
Ask & listen.
Listen to the protest songs.
Listen to the word-of-mouth truths.
Listen to the people.
Listen to the Pan-African calls to collective revolution.

Speaking in tongues

i learned to speak in many tongues. --- kiswahili. --- english.
--- punjabi. --- french. --- i would even speak hindi and write
in the sanskrit alphabet. as an adult, i no longer recall how. i
hear --- gujarati, --- spanish, --- setswana, and --- farsi, too.
those who taught me words, names, concepts, ideas, and gave
me a pencil so that i may ideate, taught me to know myself. even
as they did, they graded my assignments and wondered why
i would not obey. i was a gifted student punished for talking
too much. the teachers who taught me words but silenced my
thoughts were many. the forces to silence brown children under
the guise of making them polite and respectful were strong.
these forces both shaped me and denied me.

i learned as an adult to reclaim my voice and my words. what i
write and how i write are forms of self-claiming.
i speak in tongues.
i stitch the fractured and erased parts of myself back together
into healing cohesion. i speak myself in multiple tongues.

African-ish Ways

When folks meet me, they are often puzzled because although my body places me away from Africa, many of the unspoken ways of being i practice are connected to distinctly African values.

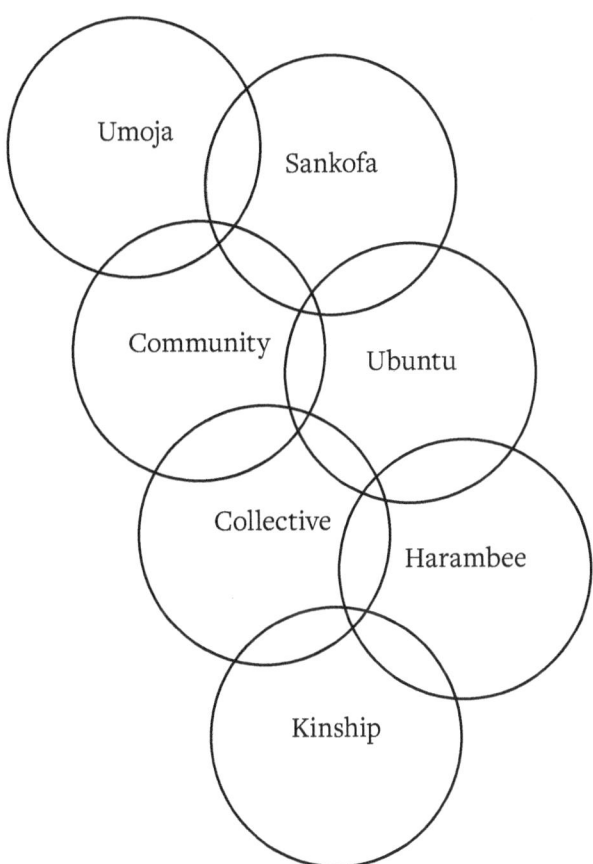

Diamonds worth

Born and raised where diamonds are mined,

I adorn my body with amber, agate, and amethyst.

I know that muti magic is crystallized.

I was taught that I am mine-rich in gems of inestimable value.

No jewel's worth compares to honesty, truth, and integrity.

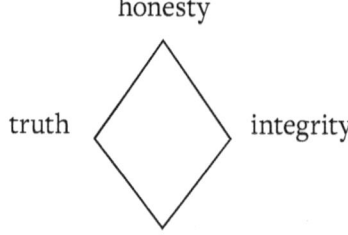

Cultural learnings

I cannot list all the learnings I internalized as a person so blessed to be born &
raised among African peoples.
I cannot fully convey the enormity of the relearning ongoing, so this is a brief remembrance—

A person is only a person among people.

Honor people. Love humanity.
Seek collectives. Be worthy of community.

Go where the people are kind, not the harvest bountiful.

Respect the land & all life.
Marvel at the glorious skies & sunsets,
bounties of nature & earth,
but if there is no community,
there is no true life.

African-ish unbelonging

To be African-ish
is to know that my father, the first immigrant to Africa in his family,
as I am the first to be born there, wished to be buried in this home.
To be African-ish is to know intimately the multiple tones
and faces and voices of xenophobia.
To be African-ish is to be a brown minority in a land colonized by
white Europeans who left a legacy of racial hierarchy in which I am
precariously placed.
To be African-ish is to be intimately acquainted with colonialism and
imperialism.

Tripod pots

When people speak of their immigrant journeys, we often say we are caught between two worlds and two languages and two cultures.
I am like the tripod pot set outside with a fire lit under it.
These are the heavy cast-iron pots with three legs holding them steady even as we fill them with metsi and motogo that we stir with wooden spoons to make our morning porridge. We gather the firewood from nearby and tend the flame under the steady but hot pot.
I feel like I am a tripod hot pot with at least three pods.

Africa is feeling

Africa is not just a place
but a feeling
healing feeling
of humanity & togetherness
impossible to explicate or replicate
                           elsewhere
                                                   anywhere.

Lost daughter

I am a lost Daughter of Africa.
My soul home, Mother Africa, is calling me today.
It is Africa Day.
In my heart, every day is Africa Day.

Mother Africa beckons me daily.
She birthed me and raised me.
She schooled me and disciplined me.

She taught me that I am a brown daughter of the continent of light.
She reminds me of my African names and tongues.

She beckons, "Nkai, wena tla kwano."
She whispers to my heart, "Almasi, kuja nyumbani . . . imekuwa muda mrefu mno."

My heart responds by overflowing through my eyes.

I feel like a lost child of Mother Africa exiled to america. Did I not choose this exile?

So many of us came here seeking freedom
pursuing education
buying into capitalist models of success.

We lost our way as we
internalized that Africa doesn't matter.

We lost our way when we started to see Africa as a dark continent and deprived ourselves of her radiant light.

We lost our way every time our accents were mocked.

We lost our way every time our humanity was micro-aggressed.

We lost our remembrance of soulful joy as we were assailed by the single story of African danger, poverty, and backwardness.

We lost ourselves as we forgot to celebrate or ululate.
We got so very lost as we inhabited those neocolonizer beliefs. We said it was survival.

We thought it was adaptation.

We weren't even conscious of losing ourselves.

DIASPORA-ISH

We separate ourselves from that true story of Africa.

We become aliens to Africa while being Aliens in america.

We suffer, often silently, the angst of Africa separation.

This is not your standard homesickness. It is
a soul wound, an illness.

My soul angst seeks for shadow comforts in bottomless cups of kahawa.

Memories of the endless flow of chai served to every guest.

I miss my folks who still reside on African soil.
I miss my Pa who is now one with Mother Africa, intermingled with her earth as he wished.

I miss hearing the soul song sounds of greetings everywhere. I miss the comfort of "Dumela, mma."

Ujambo? Habari?

Otsogile jang?

Ke la pile thata, bagaetso.
Nime choka sana hapa america.

I am soul-tired here in america.
I yearn for the humanity that is Africa.
I'll put away the kahawa now and reach for the rooibos.

Cheers to Mother Africa on any given day from a
lost daughter yearning for home.

to be African-ish is to remain quiet about Africa when diaspora wars rage on.

Diaspora debates

When diaspora Africans gather online or offline to debate:
Amapiano or Afrobeat?
Fufu or injera?
Whose dances are the best?
Whose foods are the tastiest?
Who is the Africanest of the Africanest?
Who is African enough?
i remain silent. i speak not.
i do have much to say, but i must not.
i do not question who taught us to be divided & debate as such.
i do not offer my lived experience or scholarly knowledge.

The truth to recall:
If i am African by birth,
i am not an indigenous African.
So, when diaspora debates rage among new Africans to america
& descendants of africans in the americas,
they are no concerns of mine
unless i wish to trip & fall into a fiery pit of anti-Blackness
& go down in flames with no place to call home.

Diaspora entanglements

To be a diasporic desi-ish person is to be descended from multiple displaced folks from Punjab & to be African-ish with more cultural ties to folks all over the African continent & those descended from the indentured throughout the Caribbean.

These are a few of my truthful observations about folks like me. I do not speak for us, but with & to us when I call us to reckon with our entanglements:
To be diasporic means to be constantly entangled with the machinations of imperialism. It means that we are schooled to aspire to travel, be educated in & reside in imperial cores. Even if we resist, the structures of cooptation & immigration pull us to the West or North.
We are entangled in precarious ways with empire & its ideologies.

Our dreams & aspirations are just as colonized as our pasts & lands. We are brain drained away from places we call home & culturally programmed to become successful oppressors of people just like us. We imbibe & even propagate ideas & ideologies, systems & policies that normalize our own endings.
We consent to our own tokenization & representation, confounding the latter for liberation.

When we reside in the imperial core too long, forgetting where we came from & who our people are, we become a part of it. We become agents of oppression instead of its opponents. To be diasporic is to wake up to realize that we are just as likely to become the brown/Black faces of empire as we are to become revolutionary opponents of imperialism fronting as neoliberalism. Let our waking be an unforgetting.
Let our unforgetting be a collective disentangling.
May it be a revolution.

Notes

Reflection Invitation:

What are your working definitions of and connections between the following terms or concepts?

→ **POSTCOLONIALISM & COLONIALISM**

MISSIONIZATION

→ **COLONIAL EDUCATION**

VOLUNTOURISM

→ **INTERNATIONAL DEVELOPMENT INDUSTRIAL COMPLEX**

DIASPORA·ISH

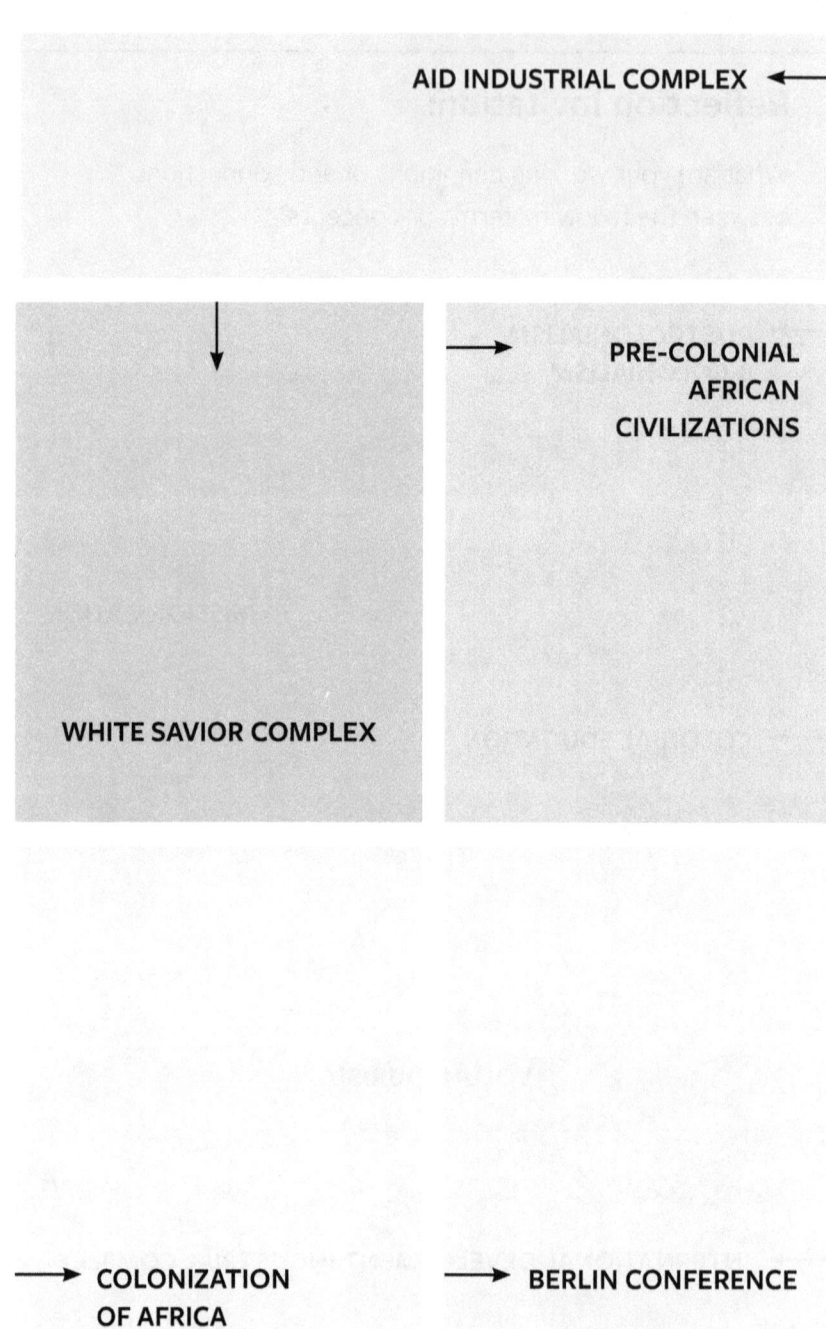

Gayatri Sethi

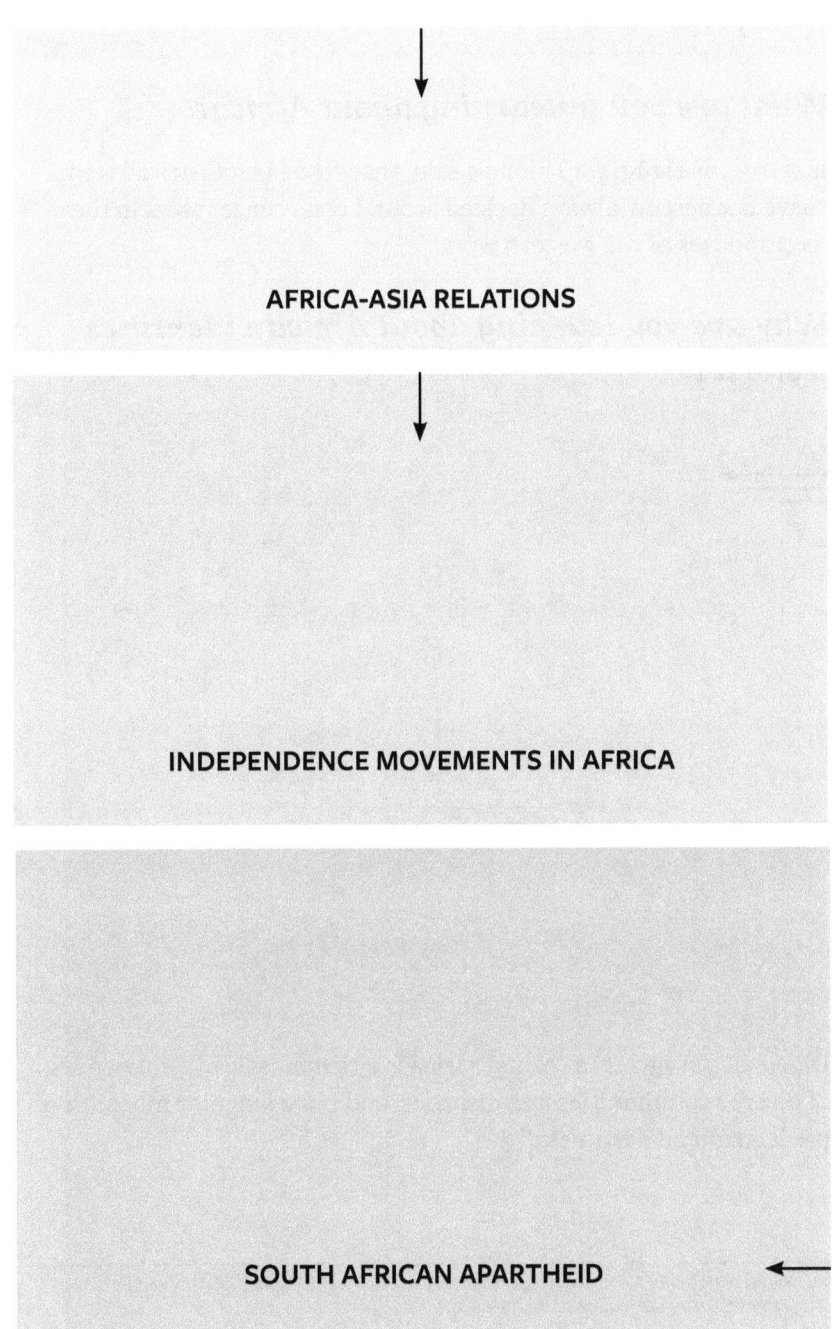

Inquiries

What are you unlearning about Africa?

Is it true, as Ngũgĩ wa Thiong'o said, that "the fate of Africa" is to "have her destiny always decided around conference tables in the metropolises of the western world"?[22]

Why are you learning about African identities & stories?

⇒

Dipo Faloyin says, "In reality, Africa is a rich mosaic of experiences, of diverse communities and histories, and not a singular monolith of predetermined destinies."[23]

---

22. Ngũgĩ wa Thiong'o, *Decolonising the Mind: The Politics of Language in African Literature* (James Currey Ltd/Heinemann, 1986), 4.

---

23. Dipo Faloyin, *Africa Is Not a Country: Notes On a Bright Continent* (W. W. Norton & Company, 2022), 18.

How are you relearning about the African diaspora?

Emigration

Re-educated

Schooling would liberate us.
Education frees, I was told.
I learned my lessons well.
I was the A-student.
I believed that this would guarantee me a freer, fuller life.
Until, upon reading the work of Paulo Freire[24], I was stunned to discover that the schooling I underwent was designed by colonizers to keep me in my place.
I was to learn of daisies and daffodils growing in prairies, meadows, and hills that I might
dream of, but never see.
I was to become one of the gatekeepers for my own.
Visa denied.
Madam, you may not enter the United Kingdom.
I had the Cambridge certificates, but was denied the diploma.
This is the ironic education of a postcolonial subject like me. We are educated to be subjugated in a world that denies our humanity.
So began an unlearning.
A re-education.
A reorientation.
I call this personal decolonization.

Immigration inquisitions

Let me tell you about the time that I made the error of speaking French to an immigration agent in Brussels.

This was 1990. I did not hold a Botswana passport then. My plane ticket sent me from Johannesburg to Brussels. An overnight layover was planned in Brussels. I had proof of an onward ticket to the united states of america. I possessed a student visa (F-1). I had enough cash

---

24. Paulo Freire, *Pedagogy of the Oppressed*, (Continuum Press, 1970).

to pay for the hotel and snacks to boot. I had planned an evening of strolling through the European city I had read about, but never visited. I intended to sample some chocolate.

Earlier that year, I had spent six weeks of language immersion in France. I had then visited Haifa and Akka in occupied Palestine for a Baha'i pilgrimage.

The immigration agent saw too many red flags to pass me through to entry.

He called over his supervisor, and in French that I understood, said that surely, I was a spy. I had an Indian passport and had just spoken to him clearly in French. The supervisor thought something of this theory, so as an eighteen-year-old, I was ushered to an inquisition room where I was questioned at length about my immigration status and where I was really from. I decided to speak in crystal clear British English. I insisted I was an eager tourist. I was an america-bound student. I was eighteen.

They saw me as a spy. They did not see me as a global traveler. They did not see me as a curious youth. They were stumped by my passport and the stamps it held.

The inquisition, with no parent to call or stranger to assist me, lasted several hours.

When I arrived at my hotel, I was too fatigued to explore. I admired the architectural beauty from afar as I suspected I would not enjoy this place up close. I smelled the stench of xenophobia lurking in European finery. Did I sample the chocolate? I do not recall. If I did, it was not memorable.

And, from such grueling experiences, repeated over a lifetime, I learned to never be too keen to speak French or reveal how much I understand to folks who hold privilege. I have now become the person

who eavesdrops on conversations in multiple languages, French, Hindi, Punjabi, Kiswahili, Setswana, even Farsi and Spanish with a straight face, not revealing my comprehension.
I do not reveal how much I follow and how much I wish to join these conversations. I listen.
I rarely, if ever, let on how much I know and where I have been.

Thanks to the immigration officers in Brussels, London, Paris, Tel Aviv,[25] & Chicago, I have also learned to disarm policing or white inquisition with finesse worthy of a spy. I also learned to interrogate immigration.

to be diasporic is to be intimately familiar with the xenophobic realities of travel & immigration.

Where they see me as one of them

I have been blessed to travel widely.
When I landed in Port of Spain, Trinidad, my soul soared.
The immigration agent glanced at me before examining my passport, and simply said the words that resounded like soul song,
"Welcome home."
I wept tears of relief and joy intermingled with awe.
How can this be?
They even pronounce my name as I wish it said, effortlessly, as if I really am known here.
I am jubilant to know that there are places in this expansive world that I might yet discover where the inhabitants see me as one of them.
Glimpses of such blending-in I have been blessed with in South Africa, throughout the Caribbean, Indian Ocean isles, Seychelles, and Mauritius.

---

25. On two separate visits to occupied Palestine, I learned firsthand what occupation and apartheid look like in the context of settler colonialism there. Many years later, I learned that the city named Tel Aviv as of 1910, where the international airport is situated, was originally named Ahuzat Bayit, near Jaffa. I prefer to use the original names of these places even though the occupation's names are most commonly used.

Consent to enter

As an adult, I learned that many Indigenous peoples all over the globe seek consent before they enter lands where they do not reside.
This is not just an ancient practice.
This is a practice I wish many immigrant settlers and travelers would adopt.
Forget a visa or work permit, what might immigration feel like if we actually asked consent to enter from the true keepers of the lands we visit or inhabit?
Consent to enter is what the call and response
"Hodi. Karibu!" signifies.

Am I a global citizen?

I no longer describe myself this way even though others might. I learned that these universal concepts are often steeped in neoliberal ideals that are white-centering.
Who is the default global citizen?
Who is excluded?
Talk of world unity & human oneness can often erase marginalized folks. Such calls for unity without addressing systemic or global inequities are harmful.
Who does global citizenship benefit?
Who is erased?

> **To be diasporic is to grapple with multiple fascist regimes threatening to deport or withdraw citizenship rights.**

Send us back

i identify as a person of the global majority.
We are the diaspora-ish global majority,
the subaltern,[26]
threatened perpetually by those invested in imperiality
with deportations, cages, incarcerations, & violences
by the ruling class de facto global minority.

If you were to send us back,
send us all back.
We dare the elected leaders,
imperial cops of all skin tones and races,
black and brown faces
in high places[27]
to send us all back.

Will you send us back to places where you bomb us?
Will you send us back to places that no longer have names?
Will you send us back to places entirely depleted by design?

Send us back if you dare,
Send us all back.

                        Land back.

Send us back to where we came from
too many places to name
to a new dimension of existence too ethereal to fathom.

---

26. Subaltern, a term coined by Antonio Gramsci, refers to the oppressed working class in a capitalist system. I use it as do many postcolonial studies scholars (notably Gayatri Spivak in her 1988 essay "Can The Subaltern Speak?") to refer to groups excluded from structures of citizenship in postcolonial times.

---

27. Ruha Benjamin, "Ruha Benjamin - Spelman Convocation 2024," April 11, 2024, posted April 16, 2024, by Outspoken Agency, YouTube, 14:55, https://www.youtube.com/watch?v=j_12_E3LAeg&ab_channel=OutspokenAgency.

Send us back to time before colonialism.
Though we do not idealize the before, we imagine another, freer after.
Send us forward to a timeline,
a time warp
free of colonial borders, colonial occupations, colonial extractions.

Land back.

If you send us backwards and forwards in time & space,
we will not shatter,

                like shards of a broken empire.
                We, the scattered,
                like seeds, will scatter,
                freer,
                freer,
                and freer.

DIASPORA·ISH

*Many questions arise when speaking of displaced
& dispossessed peoples.*

Fourth World

There is no other world for those from the third world[28]
residing in first world
now being told to return.
The stateless, the foreign, foreigners everywhere,
will need to be deported teleported
through a portal
to another, new new,
not fourth world.
Intergenerationally displaced,
we are not indigenous to any one place.

*Some of us have no watan homelands to return to
or no right of return.*

---

28. The oft-used term Third World is one to study and reframe. It is part of a colonial and racist hierarchy of the world. Sometimes, it is reclaimed as a political identity to refer to oppressed nations resisting imperialism. Fourth World, another outdated term, encompasses the most marginalized peoples of the world (including nomads and Indigenous peoples).

No return

Where in the world will the sender send
asylum seekers, refugees, exiles & diasporic others,

the ajnabi अजनबी | أَجْنَبِي | اجنب

dispossessed by empire
displaced   by Nakba, border violence,
not of their own making
unless there is a right of return?

Return to sender.
Return the right to return.
The sender stole our right to return.
The sender stole.
There is no return to sender.[29]

The us/them of diaspora is unclear when we, diasporic folks, become proponents of exclusionary politics.

---

29. Ajnabi is a word that has multiple meanings. I have heard it used to signify "foreigner" or "settler" even as it might imply those who are estranged from their lands.

AMERICAN·ISH

My coming to america

Many of us who enter the united states learn the code words & legalities of immigration quickly. F-1. H-1B. Green card. Naturalized citizen.
Immigrants often pay attention to the nuances & differences in the types of immigration journeys, choices & realities among us. Those who call us immigrants assume a uniformity of experience that is often elusive.
Those who weaponize words like immigrant rarely fully comprehend immigration history or policies.
What we often fail to come to terms with is how we folks from the majority world, from the two-thirds world, often misnamed Third World, are consumed & co-opted by the american empire. Some political theorists have named this as the periphery within the center.
People like me are the margins & peripheries existing within the centers of empire.[30]
Much of my life on american soil is deeply informed by an entanglement with white supremacy.
Many of the folks who immigrate here become white-adjacent. I could be. I have been at times.
From the moment I landed in the united states, I recognized familiar forms of colonization and apartheid here.
I recognize a settler-colonial state fronting as a self-professed democracy.
The pressures to become white-adjacent remain omnipresent.
I continue to resist. When we arrive, model minority myths are sold & fed to us. These stories constrain us. They indoctrinate us into assimilation while othering us into oppression.
We are required to translate & transmute ourselves even as we must build ourselves into bridges for others to cross over to see, recognize & know us.

---

[30]. These are references to terms that are often used to describe relations of imperialism. This is an invitation to research center-periphery.

Re-entry to america

I land in Houston after taking a group of my undergraduate students to Trinidad for a cultural immersion trip. I do not fly with a U.S. passport. Though I have recently experienced the ease of arriving in Port of Spain & blending in, I am still prepared for a different kind of welcome in Houston. Head covered, I approach the immigration officer with a bright smile & greeting. Batswana taught me well that greeting is a way of seeing humanity & there are no strangers in life if we greet each other with a nod or part with a blessing. I imagine singing, "Dumela, rra." But instead I offer up my passport with a simple smile.

The invented categories in immigration forms have real consequences. The officer pauses. It is a long pause.

He glances at me. He glances at the passport.

"Earth calling Houston," I say in jest in my head.
Oh, yes, I am oriented. I have arrived in Houston & I cannot wait to return to Atlanta to hug my children again after a long week of constant teaching.
After what seems like an extended examination of my documents—green card scanned, my photo taken—I am asked to present my hands for fingerprinting.

I comply.

I do not have passport privilege. I am accustomed to such inquisitions in airports.
Trinidad truly was a relief. No extra red tape. No visa needed. No proof of funding.
Welcome home?
I will not receive this greeting here. I know this.
The agent raises his eyebrows after all the formality and inquires, "Where is Botswana?"

I am a teacher. I am an educator. My knee-jerk response is to throw a question back at him. He is a federal employee charged with weighty decisions about who enters U.S. borders. Shouldn't he know basic world geography?
This is america. He has no clue. Before I can swallow my humor, I invite him to guess.

He stares back with no humor & no conjecture.
The pause is long until I inform him that I could not help my teacher instincts & yes, I am a brown African because Botswana is a southern African nation.
He does not blink. He does not smile. He simply hands me back my passport & green card (to my relief) & states, "I have never seen one of these before."
I exhale. I sigh. I do not allow him to see me cringe. americans, do your homework.
I'm feeling quite like an alien again. Still.
So many inquisitions & interrogations leave me depleted.
So many looks & stares find me exhausted.
Do I seek citizenship as passport privilege as a respite?
I do not.

Immigrant trauma responses

> Roxane Gay asks
> "How do we write trauma?"[31]

Before I read her thoughtful interview, I jot down:

Slowly. Mindfully. Tenderly. Compassionately.

For me, writing potentially traumatic experiences of unbelonging requires keeping things general & vague. I refuse to regurgitate every slap in the face or instance of discrimination. Some psychologists say that retelling trauma creates more trauma. Often, we repeat the cycles instead of interrupting them. I write my trauma vaguely, slowly, cautiously.

These are some of my immigrant trauma responses:

Hiding identities can be a trauma response to othering & oppression. When some of our identities conflict with each other, then we adapt and hide them to get by. But when this becomes a way of life, a forgetting of sorts, we lose vital parts of ourselves. This happens to me.

How do we recoup our lost selves? Or, do we go adrift? I have often gone adrift.

Those of us taught by colonized education to stay on a narrow path to acceptability, respectability & success, often confuse systemic inequities with personal failures. Success by colonial standards can be an immigrant trauma response. I have been on this path, but also escaped it.

Where unjust systems meet personal growth, I pitch an unwieldy tent.

I dwell there.

---

31. Roxane Gay, "Roxane Gay on How to Write About Trauma," interview by Monica Lewinsky, Vanity Fair, February 18, 2021, https://www.vanityfair.com/style/2021/02/roxane-gay-on-how-to-write-about-trauma.

Immigrations

Global migration crisis

Without genocidal land grabs, without imperial or proxy wars, would there be mass human dispossessions, displacements, disorientations of immigration?
Do we name the reasons some of us are made into asylum seekers or refugees?
It must be stated that without imperial border regimes, in the absence of colonial violences, in a world without genocides, we would have no "immigration crisis."
In the absence of a climate crisis, itself an outcome of ongoing imperialism, there would be no migration crisis.
We are made into a crisis.
Migrants are not the problem or the crisis.
What are the roots of this crisis?

What if immigration debates & politics were resituated?

I often exclaim:

america is a helluva ride.
Every time a new injustice unfolds, I say:
america is on-brand.
american-brand capitalism sucks my life force.
Every now & again, I awake to dismay:
america is a dumpster fire.

The pages that follow are my ride on these lands.
I've been knotted up, exhausted, oppressed & traumatized while learning, hopeful, protesting & audacious.
There are struggle songs & protest verses.
There are lessons & blessings.

The oppressive political system of the united states of america is described by bell hooks as:
Imperialist white-supremacist capitalist patriarchy.[32]

Audre Lorde teaches:
There is no such thing as a single-issue struggle because we do not live single-issue lives.[33]

To be an american-ish immigrant is to live & breathe daily with weighty questions & reminders that belonging is unbelonging in belonging.

To be here is to reside on the land whose keepers are the Mvskoke.[34] But as an immigrant, I was almost forty years old when I first heard this land acknowledgement.

To be here is to be educated & to hold multiple degrees from elite institutions that pride themselves on their global acclaim.

To be here is to know that I hold considerable educational privilege while being minoritized & presumed inadequate despite my verifiable advanced global competence.

To be here is also to be keenly aware that brown people end up in cages & on the other side of walls.

---

32. bell hooks, *Feminism is for Everybody: Passionate Politics* (South End Press, 2000), 46.

---

33. Lorde, "Learning from the 60s", 138.

---

34. Muscogee and Mvskoke are spellings for the Creek nation in the southeast united states where I reside.

What are you?

How come you are African but you say you are not African-American? What is Apartheid?
Would you consider running for public office? I assumed you were american. Don't you act like an american? Where are you really from? What's a critical language? Why do you even live in the U.S.? What's an F-1? Don't you have a green card? You're set then, right?
Why didn't you just get naturalized to be an american? Why don't you celebrate Christmas? How does the travel ban even affect you? What does being a Bahá'í have to do with the countries on the travel ban list? So does that mean you're actually Muslim? Why do you sometimes cover your head? What is wrong with being a migrant? Aren't you a migrant? What does "mother of Black children" even mean? If you're not american & you can't vote, why can't you contact your senators, anyway? What are you, anyway?

Inquiry is not inquisition

If they think they know me, chances are they've been assuming quite a bit & hardly know me at all.

When asked sincerely, I'm happy to answer these questions & tell them some stories, too.

The relentless questions are an inquisition. My answers to these questions:

I'm the kind of other who could very easily & for many different reasons end up on a list or on the other side of a wall.

I am not alone.

There are many others just like me. We are not exceptions.

Words can be weaponized to exclude and other.

Words for others

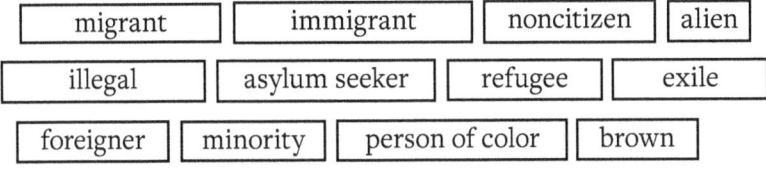

They use these words like weapons to separate, divide, remove & end us.

What we are called here:

    brown

        South Asian

            South Asian American

                desi

Even if we are seen or represented as a monolith, we contain multitudes.
We are from Bangladesh, Sri Lanka & Nepal.
They assume we are all Indian.
We are of many castes & faiths.
They assume we are all Hindu.

We are imagined as wealthy, white-adjacent, playing tennis at our homes in the suburbs.
They see doctors, lawyers, professors, not taxi drivers, bodega workers, dishwashers.
They see & tell a single myth of success.

When I speak of us "desis" or "brown folks," I am hinting at both the collective identity of brown desiness, but also seek to question how our stories are compiled into a single story.

I am learning that when we are unsure about identity, we should ask folks how they would prefer to be identified. Call them by the affiliations they choose, rather than place the burdens of external affiliations on them.

Human dictionary

No dictionary definitions are required.
I know these words as experiential vocabulary

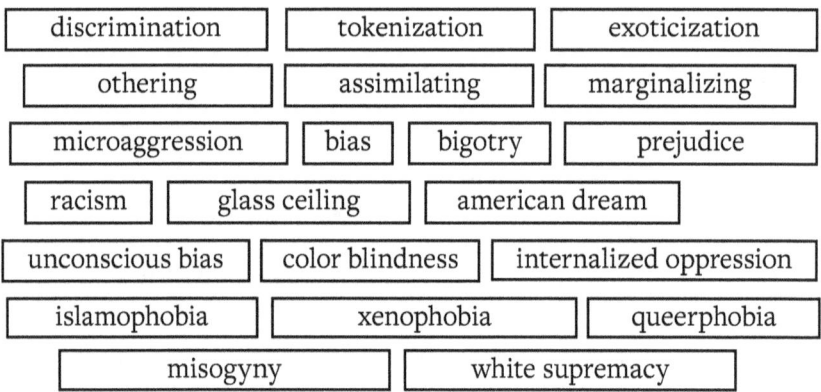

Some may require a dictionary.
I am a living breathing surviving
illustrated exemplified
dictionary of -isms personified.

I am also a human diary
whose pages are overflowing
with courage, resilience,
means to cope,

will to hope
& resistance
to -isms.

I is for immigrant

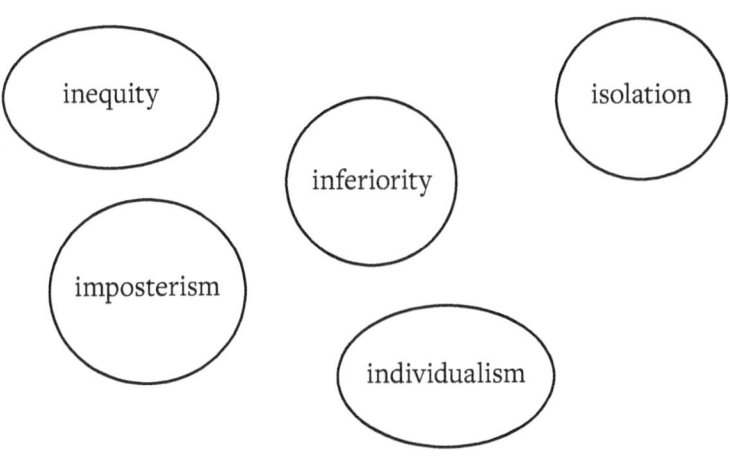

to be American-ish is to reframe common refrains.

We are not marginal.
We are marginalized.

We are not minority.
We are minoritized.

> **We are People of the Global Majority.**

Othering is dehumanizing

Us   Us
Us   belong
Us   here
Us   human

Us   them
Citizens   Non-citizens
Immigrants
Illegals
Undocumented

un-belong
un-human?

Othering makes us versus them.
Othering builds

Walls
Borders
Separations.
Othering
Confines
Violates
Kills.
Othering
Dehumanizes while justifying a
falsely constructed US.

There are no others when we are all human.

Immigrant explanations

I am weary.
Immigration is often a privilege.
Those who only see a brown body do not care how I came to be here.
It is also true: to those unfamiliar, who care less for distinction, is there a difference between a South Asian & a Central American?
If DHS decided to deport one of us, would documentation or immigration status matter?
      Maybe.
      Maybe not.

Immigrant invisibility

americans who aren't americans
We the immigrants
We live here
We work here
We might even bear children who are from here
But we are always the "other"
Ever ever the other
We don't get to belong here
We are erased from belonging
& we do not have any other place to call home
americans who aren't americans

We are here
Maybe we seek to belong here
But, we are neither here nor there
We are other
We are ether
We are vapor

Here.
Not here.
You see?

We are invisible & hyper-visible
americans who aren't americans
We the immigrants are sort of visible &
even so, you seek to erase or remove us.

> *Questions around types of immigration get slippery when immigrants classify or police each other.*

To those who seek to remove us,
does it matter if we are documented or undocumented?
Does legality matter?
Are citizenship rights even real?
Does it matter why or how we came here?
(South) Asians end up incarcerated, deported, or in cages, too,
you know.
Oppression Olympics are not going to free us, though.
How do we redress xenophobia & seek justice in immigration for
us all?

Immigrant code switching

is the mode of linguistic & cultural
survival of those immigrants
perpetually stereotyped & othered
in every space we enter.
We learn to adapt & become
shapeshifters in ways that leave
us wondering who or how we truly are.

Spelling "BE" while Indian

what does it mean to be
class privileged-supposed-model-minority-while-always-other in america?
you could spell.
win the Spelling Bee (like a boss)
stand off against another Indian who
spells like a boss, too
either way, we win (or so we think) for
the umpteenth year in a row
you spell like it's your very life that depends on it you
could master the Master's tongue
better than his progeny
you could educate smudge-ucate yourself up by
the bootstraps
like you were told
   you could train to spell
like you were a professional athlete
get those eyes on the prize
study study study
work work work
& still be
belittled
be dismissed
be invisible
be mocked
"We are just kidding" they say
"Joke's on you"
"Your A's don't count"
"Study all you want"
"Your win ain't no big deal"
"You can try to win the Bee"
"But you just can't BE."
It's already been decided by the powers that be.

Ungrateful immigrant

I am called an ungrateful immigrant.
Because I do not celebrate america.

They say I am unpatriotic.
Why are you even here?
Go back where you came from.
America has never loved

                    the Indigenous
            the enslaved & their descendants
                      the brown
                  the immigrants
                    the Muslims
                or the LGBTQ+

america will never love
us
the marginalized
the terrorized
the invisible & erased
who make america
america
has always been an imperial
fascist state perpetrating genocides.
Peddling superiority & promises of
freedoms.
Lies masking oppressions manifold.
To speak these truths is
to be told
you are unwelcome here.

We already knew
but we are here anyway.
Telling truth & resisting injustice are

the ultimate patriotism.
Didn't you know?
We know.

> *To be diasporic is to imagine immigrant unity in diaspora.*

Immigrant misfit

I often wonder, "what is the matter with me that I do not belong?" Even in a land considered a melting pot, place of dreams, I am a misfit.

> I have never pledged allegiance to the flag.
> I do not stand for the national anthem.
> I am not enamored of the star spangled banner.

These doubts were born of the taunts that plagued my youth. These were the unsung struggle songs of my heart and soul. I wonder and I wander.

> *To belong here requires repeated assimilation.*

Truths about america for all times

This is a settler colony on stolen land built on genocides of indigenous peoples & labor of the enslaved. This is not a nation of immigrants.[35] america is a global force of imperialism. Its flag is the most burnt flag in the world. This flag is a symbol of colonialism globally.

---

35. Roxane Dunbar-Ortiz, *Not A Nation of Immigrants: Settler Colonialism, White Supremacy, and a History of Erasure and Exclusion* (Beacon Press, 2021).

Refuse nationalism

I am deeply distrusting of nationalism & patriotism. I participate in my own unbelonging by refusing to become a naturalized U.S. citizen, choosing precarity in the form of visa & permanent residence applications that are subject to expiration. I have sometimes been "documented." I have often been policed for documentation. I do not intend to be more sucked into american imperialism than I already am. I have resided here for more than half my life. How does it matter whether I hold a visa or a green card? And yet, I am keenly aware that documentation might not protect me from being repressed, disappeared, or deported. To avoid becoming a settler immigrant, to the surprise of many, I also refuse to hold passports or own property in the sacred lands where I reside.
Land back to me means that I do not uphold citizenship myths. I do not own land.

Abolish America

why I say america or amerikkka not America

Abolish the very idea of America
empire fronting as freedom
america not America
awesomely affluent
stolen land
erasing indigenous life & sovereignty
america is all lives mattering
while anti-Black by design
america is no dream
as it builds walls on unceded lands to cage children it imagines as migrants
america is god bless america but the atm is god

america is ammunition aimed at its own children
no gun control but book bans proliferate
no free speech no abortions
also unfree
america is inherently lethal
all of us
upholding its unfreedoms
as we fly flags
that symbolize
all the world's demise.

My american dream

In the united states of america, immigrants who enter with no nuanced knowledge of the history of this nation's settler colonialism & white supremacy are bound to become new settlers. We erase the histories of Indigenous & Black folks as we settle here on lies sold as american dreams of better living. There are no dreams here. I came with dreams of higher education & plans to return to the lands of the Tswana or Sotho or Zulu. I did not dream to stay. I dreamed of a life of seva & tirelo to the peoples who invited us expats to become naturalized citizens. I dreamed of learning skills that I would pack into my brain.
I would contain my life into two suitcases (twenty kilos each) to carry homeward. Was I cautioned that I would get trapped here? I do not recall. Perhaps, I did not heed the warnings. My american dream was to leave america as soon as I possibly could.
Every now & then, I dream this dream as I curse the forces that keep me here year after year.

It dawns on me one day as I ponder who signifies safety for my family that if we live segregated lives in gentrified spaces, it is highly unlikely that our sanctuaries are integrated.

If they come for us, where will we go?

I woke up today to danger on the horizon.
The election loomed & a wave of white supremacy stormed the Capitol.
Re-elections happened & a new wave of hysteria about rising fascism erupted.
        Deportations. Protests against deportations.

If they come for us, where would we go?[36]
We would not go to the white neighbors who have not nodded to us in the four years we lived next door. We eye their "Black Lives Matter" signs in the yard, but we would not dare knock on their door.
Where would we go?
There is no gurudwara nearby, or we would flee there. There is no Black Church nearby, or else, we would, like baba's grandfather years ago, also seek refuge there. There are no Black or brown families or chosen kin nearby, or else we might find them & offer them solace, too. Grandmommy has passed on or else we would find our way to her. She rests, we hope in peace & I wonder if we could go to her resting place for refuge to offer prayers there. Our closest friends who are chosen kin are too far away in Raleigh & Chicago & New York & Gaborone & Paris, too. My son chimes in that we are our own refuge. We will need to encourage one another to brave whatever comes.

        When they come for us, where will we flee for safety?
        Who signifies safety? Who do I include in my "us"?

What capitalism & patriarchy & whiteness have taught us about safety is untrue. Being "the only" renders us vulnerable. Being "exceptional" in acceptability offers no safety.
We know that our people—brown, Black & gold[37]—are our safety.
We know that to be people—bold, never bought & sold—is our safety.
Where they live, we ought to be.

---

36. Fatimah Asghar, "If They Should Come For Us," Poetry Foundation, March 2017, https://www.poetryfoundation.org/poetrymagazine/poems/92374/if-they-should-come-for-us.

---

37. Asghar, "If They Should . . ."

Educations

Many marginalized folks refer to university campuses as modern-day plantations. In the mouths of whiteness, sending us back to the plantation is a weaponized reality.

F-1

International Student
Non-immigrant
deemed worthy of entering the
US of A to study.
But first i need to pass the TOEFL.
Test of English as a Foreign Language.
You may not enter on
an F-1 visa
unless you pass this test.

Do U.S. students take this test?
Of course not.
They speak English. Which English?
i speak desi English, British English, South African English.
But, i will need to learn american English to be admitted here.

Plus, we have extra hurdles.
International students need to prove
that we have enough cash in the bank to pay our way
because we are less likely to be eligible for funding.
We might even subsidize the education of those
who speak american English.
F-1
We might know this yet:
the University is still a plantation.[38]

We might need to learn this quickly.
No bootstrap myth,
no assimilation tricks,
no faith in the so-called "american dream"
will prepare us for the F-1 life
of indentured servitude
on the university plantation.
We might even deny this
& suffer in silence
Because we were told
when we applied & were granted the sought after
F-1
to be grateful & obedient
for the opportunity
to pay tuition
while being exploited, silenced & oppressed
by systemic xenophobia & isms countless.
Be glad & grateful to be an
F-1
on this plantation.
If we are attentive,
we might learn that our dismal reality
is considerably or marginally
better off than
Black
Indigenous
Muslim
& undocumented folks.
We might slip & fall into plantation life
by becoming complicit in oppressions of others.
We might be tricked into belief that proximity
to powerful will earn us a free pass

---

38. Kehinde Andrews, "I Compared Universities to Slave Plantations to Disturb, Not Discourage," The Guardian, October 24, 2016, https://www.theguardian.com/commentisfree/2016/oct/24/universities-slave-plantations-racist.

but alas, F-1, non-immigrant,
student, conditionally here, be grateful.
Speak English, obey the rules,
or go back to where you came from.

Spaces & places where I have learned & labored

University of Chicago
Stanford University
Spelman College
Agnes Scott College

& countless campuses
where I am invited as a
guest speaker or
consultant.

Safe & brave spaces

Much of my time in the united states has been spent either as a learner or educator in higher education spaces. These spaces, I was told, were liberal havens of tolerance & intellectual freedom. Safe spaces are often unsafe for me.

I learned repeatedly at university campuses where I studied & labored that white supremacy thrives there. Under the guise of diversity or inclusion, these institutions of higher learning perpetuate power hierarchies & imbalances. I was taught curricula that centered whiteness as normative. I was expected to teach these so-called classics. I even pursued fields of study like anthropology & sociology only to uncover that they are in fact whiteness studies. To earn a PhD from an elite university, as I did, is to become an expert in whiteness. These spaces of learning claim to be safe for inquiry. The inconsistencies between the claims of higher education & the realities of relentless discrimination & mistreatment of brown and Black folks resulted in academic trauma for me.

My speech was not free. My inquiries & utterances led me to become a problem. I was deemed difficult, disruptive & even defiant.[39] My outspoken activism was unwelcome. When I declined being used as a face of diversity while being silenced in private offices by supervisors, my unbelonging in these not-so-safe spaces was complete. I found relentless erasures from my peers & colleagues who envied my outspokenness even as they conspired to remove me from their spaces. The condition of my welcome was my complicity. I often wondered why my critical inquiries & decolonial approaches were shunned or resisted. I questioned myself.

I lost my sense of self-worth as I wandered through the pitfalls of erasure & fell in the traps of diversity initiatives. I eventually learned to own my own voice & reclaim myself.
This shift meant that I rejected the very premises of my conditional presence on college campuses. There are no safe spaces in the Ivory Tower for folks like me.

The whiteness of (university) is Jim Crow, new style.[40]
The way forward is treacherous. If I am serious in my desire to decolonize, I must endlessly reckon with what I was taught & what I learned as normative during my time in "higher" education.

I have much to unlearn. The very behaviors I practiced to get by in academia are survival tactics that become oppressive. Integrity called

---

39. "If you expose a problem, you pose a problem." Ahmed, 18.

---

40. Cornel West, "Cornel West: The Whiteness of Harvard and Wall Street Is 'Jim Crow, New Style," interview by George Yancy, Truthout, March 5, 2021 https://truthout.org/articles/cornel-west-the-whiteness-of-harvard-and-wall-street-is-jim-crow-new-style/.

my name. I forgive my former self for not knowing what I know now. We need brave spaces to unlearn, relearn & begin again.

Fields of study

When I came to study overseas, my aim was to return home with expertise that would contribute to "advancement" or "progress" there.
Some of my areas of inquiry, learning & ongoing study (in which I hold multiple degrees) are: politics, international relations, public policy, international education, global studies, comparative feminisms, international development, youth resistance movements, African Studies, postcolonial studies, and so on and on.
Every time I realized that a discipline was colonial, I abandoned it to pursue interdisciplinarity or criticality.
Now, I rarely claim expertise.
I have no disciplinary home.
My academic unbelonging is a form of precarity.

Academic unbelonging

For almost two decades of my life, I considered college campuses home-like. I was lulled by their quirky charms & architecture. I was lured in by their fancy gardens & manicured landscapes. I was attracted to the energy of youth & curiosity.
I was sucked into the majestic libraries. I was embraced by the silent promises of knowledge. I enjoyed wielding the ID cards & keys to basement libraries. I relished hauling stacks of books & notebooks from one classroom to the next. I imagined that nobody would question my presence there. I earned access to Greek lettered societies with secret handshakes. I would fade into the scenery. I was consoled by predictable practices. I was willing to overlook the slights

& dismissals. I had faith in my own studiousness. I later realized that I had so much of my worth & identity tied up in scholarship & being an educator. These identities stifled me.
I am no longer drawn to college campuses. I no longer belong there. I do not identify as an academic.

Discriminated while degreed

We are misled into placing our self-esteem & worth on awards & degrees. We over identify with degrees and mistake them for identities. We experience the daily indignities of discrimination while degreed. We deteriorate.

On being an aunty professor

I contracted many ailments while other in academia.
PTSD.
Migraines.
Severe vertigo.
Autoimmune disorders.
Imposter syndrome.
Panic attacks.
Insomnia.
All these ailments paled in comparison to the
abuse in the form of
the push & pull
that resulted in
a simultaneous parading of my body while
I was subtly
silenced
undermined

discounted
told I was not enough.
I died an academic death
from a thousand cuts that
led to a lay-off.
With all the outward diversity touting posturing
that claimed that those embodied as
other
as me
were welcome on campus,
the ailment that I contracted
while employed as an alternative track academic was the
deep-seated academic precarity
that comes from outward valuation while
being covertly erased.
Laid off.
I was erased.
I was removed.
I was expelled.
I was exiled.
The higher-ups claimed, "This lay-off is not a reflection of
your work."
I knew my worth &
I knew the work
invisible to most
that went into sustaining my wholeness.
I left
with a severe case of academic PTSD
and a case of academic precarity
in which diversity is valued but
I am erased.
If it were not for the hundreds of
former students
who bemoaned aloud my academic death & still
call me "aunty" or "professor"

I'd be completely undone.
So I live on to heal in exile
away from academia to
reconcile myself
with my worth and work.

Academic exiles

Countless realizations & ongoing reckonings keep me exiled away from academia.
University is the third pillar of empire.[41]
Universities built on stolen lands, no matter how
diverse, are highly inequitable spaces designed to culturally program participants into compliance, not liberation. As much as classrooms are proclaimed to be liberatory spaces & colleges deemed progressive, the actual work of educating is not unlike that of policing.
What happens when students protest on campuses?
What transpires when learners demand universities disclose & divest from genocide-supporting sources of funding?
How is free speech not free at universities overridden with repression?
The inherently violent structures of universities are manifest for all the world to behold:
When universities arrest & evict their students for protesting, withhold their degrees instead of awarding them for liberating, every university campus might as well be a Cop City.
Those who fully grasp the implications of these realities, wishing no longer to be complicit, must reckon with becoming exiled.
Is it possible to salvage the work of learning from the imperial designs of universities?
There are those who believe in the possibility of reforming universities from within.

---

41. Craig Steven Wilder, *Ebony & Ivory: Race, Slavery, and the Troubled History of America's Universities* (Bloomsbury Press, 2013).

But, it is my understanding based on decades of struggling, that it is not possible to salvage universities from their foundations in white supremacy.
I am an academic exile, by design, but not by choice.

Black feminists & abolitionists taught me

bell hooks. Audre Lorde. Toni Morrison. Ntozake Shange. June Jordan. Assata Shakur. Maya Angelou. Toni Cade Bambara. Brittney Cooper. Emily Caruthers. adrienne maree brown. Moya Bailey. Kimberlé Crenshaw. Bettina Love. Angela Davis. Mariame Kaba. Joy James. Alexis Pauline Gumbs. (the list must go on & on)
My students, friends, kindred & sistren.

Black feminists & abolitionists are my intellectual influencers.
I listen to their teachings & their feelings.
I witness, in their work, truths that my colonial
education hid from me.

Even if academia miseducated me, it also offered learnings in liberation.

Countless life lessons were taught to me in relationships, not in places of learning.

Black folks taught me.
Their words were balms,
a soothing kind of liberation.
The more I read them,
the more my sore self
wounded by my precarious sense of self
uplifted myself by speaking to myself
with gentle care & radical truth.
They inspire my inclinations for
affirmation & collective action.

Even as i cite & offer credit to the people who have taught me, i realize that it is an unjust predicament that Black folks guide us even as we harm them.

I vow to do better.

In these liberatory words,
I feel seen.
I have a place.
I imagine possibility.
I practice creativity.
I inhabit the margins.
I build bridges there.

Cautionary note: I have no words to convey the need for nuance when speaking of Black folks. There are so many toxic tropes that constrain their humanity. If I am not careful, I might slip & harm them even as I try to thank them.

Asante tupu haijai chungu. Empty thanks do not fill the pot.

Identities and Unbelongings

For us, living as American-ish folks, our identities often overlap, play, intersect & disconnect in complex ways. What are my lived experiences, anecdotes, observations & learnings about identities & belongings in diaspora?

Polycultural

i am an american-ish
who grew up on the African continent
spelling color with a u as colour
& splendor as splendour.

i adapted my accents &
my spelling
in the days before spell check.

i am not just polylingual,
i am polycultural.

Even in English, the language in
which i was schooled,
i switch codes between
southern African
Hinglish
southern american.

Our home

This home we are building is a fortress of well-being.
We leave our shoes at the door. We wash our hands first thing. When we enter, there is light & a faint hint of cumin in the air. We eat on fading tablecloths purchased long ago from Victoria Falls.
We are surrounded by treasures & trinkets from our travels.
Our books are piled throughout the house.
We are always reminded of our family all over the world. It is always Black History Month over here.
The aroma of fresh lit incense & coffee brewing wakes us.
We listen to jazz with baba & the beats of bhangra with mama.
Any given Saturday, we might hear kirtan intermingled with Farsi chants of Bahá'í prayers.

Multi-identified

On religious holy days, Eid, Naw-Ruz or Diwali, we remember, but rarely celebrate.
On Sundays, we Whatsapp Nani and sometimes Mamu, too.
We eat pakoras with chai on rainy days.
We crave mama's daal when we need comfort.
We hear Hindi, Spanish & Setswana.
We dream of Botswana night skies.
We plan travels to new places where we might be perceived to belong.
We speak the language of virtues & translate the boli of justice.
We pray our home is a sanctuary.

Unbelonging is our vibe

Those of us fluent in the language of belonging, comprehend that silence, pauses, tone, inflection are just as potent in signaling belonging or unbelonging as words themselves.

American racism

To be american-ish is
to confess
that this land is obsessed
with race.
Racism is the single most pressing
-ism
To be american-ish
is to become desensitized
and dehumanized.
To be american-ish
is to be the brown desi-ish
mother of Black children.
This demands that you
unlearn a lot of what
you were taught
about respectability politics.
To be american-ish is
to realize
that there is an unspoken
expectation
to conform, adapt & assimilate.
Refusing to do so comes
at tremendous risk.

Who is Blindian? Blasian?

These are relatively new terms used to describe my family. In our family, one parent is Black and another is from the Indian/Asian subcontinent. My children of both desi and Black heritage may be called Blindian or Blasian.

Parenting Black children while brown

When my daughter was three, a child she was playing with informed her that she did not play with brown-skinned girls. When my children informed me of this, I went to her teacher who informed me that my child was mistaken. It happened again & then again. At the same school, a few years later, my son was called the n-word by his classmates. When he reported it to the teacher, she accused him of fabricating the situation for attention.

When it happened again & I intervened, these teachers defended the other children & accused my child of multiple transgressions. In this ongoing parenting journey, on the job, I learned that anti-Blackness begins early. By the time they were in first grade, both my children had faced the n-word directed at them. The deep-seated denial by educators & white parents of these realities are oppressive.

I paid tuition to an elite school that valued time in nature, hikes & woodwork but conversations around race were deemed divisive. Those targeted by racism had no recourse. Every attempt to redress these harms was met with denial or worse.

I resorted to amplifying conversations in our home, in earnest, about race & identity. I could not prepare or shield my children for what we might encounter in classrooms, baseball fields, gardens, & even friends' homes, but I could be sure that they understood who they are & how to not to internalize the -ism projected onto them because of their skin color. In our home, we talk often & openly about racism. We take pride in our blended identities. We advocate for our Black kin. We defend our humanity by refusing to enter spaces where our spirits are harmed.

We do not sugarcoat the hurtful truths & we always affirm ourselves. We now homeschool. We aim to raise free Black people who are never presumed unworthy. We aim to bypass the school-to-prison pipeline where our children are already systemically & historically set up to fail. We eschew old-school colonial forms of discipline. We recoil at the capitalist oppressions that seep into our humanity. We recognize that many of the institutions where we seek support, in fact, soul-wound our children & youth.
These choices & decisions marginalize us further from mainstream american culture. We struggle. There are few safe spaces for folks like us.
We persist. This is how we humanize.

america is amerikkka

amerikkka?
This is amerikkka
dystopia.
My children and I bear witness to
systemic violence
against Black & brown humanity.
A simple brunch outing, just down the street will
make us witness to
    racist systemic violence
police encounters all for
    traffic stops
assaulting our Black & brown kin into
fearful submission.
We cry out in dismay as
our children say

Mama, I'm so scared.
Mom, the police are being rough.

He didn't even do anything.
Why are they cuffing him?
Dad, don't take a picture!
Baba, you'll get in trouble, too.
What if they come for you?
Mama, I want to leave here right now.
Child, don't look the other way.

We need to be here.
We can't run from this.
I see your fear.
As I see the fear in the eyes of the stranger cuffed & manhandled by
the police.
   Traffic stop.
Child, breathe. Stay calm.
Be ready in case we need to approach the scene.
Child, we are here to witness.
Hold my hand.
Your father is cursing.
Your brother is now in a funk. Mysteriously,
your mother's chronic pain is searing sharply
through her gut.

You know what else I see?
Cafe full of
white folks enjoying their poached eggs waffles
& sipping their iced tea.
Unstirred.
Unmoved by the scene.
Not one of them bats an eye as
the encounter unfolds.
They do not see
what we see.
They do not bear witness
to trauma by systemic violence.

They sip tea
& fantasize out loud about going to yoga tonight. No lie.
Child, I can talk to you about the police racism
systemic violence.
   Traffic stops.
But, I have no words to help you cope comprehend
or grapple
with white silence
disdain.
apathy
in the face of Black and brown pain.

Cautionary notes

Do not collapse brown immigrant status with the real lived experiences of your Black partner and children. Work diligently to draw the distinctions. Strive not to overclaim their experiences as if they were yours.
But, notice when we move through traffic stops & public spaces as a unit—as a family—their experiences are also yours.

Soul-wounding

Bettina Love writes about the spirit murdering[42] of Black and brown youth in American schools. I coined the phrase "soul-wounding" to convey the ways we are wounded by identity policing.

Those who police our identities with their words & attitudes & rules & policies
soul-wound us.

---

42. Bettina Love, "How Schools Are 'Spirit Murdering' Black and Brown Students," Education Week, May 24, 2019, https://www.edweek.org/leadership/opinion-how-schools-are-spirit-murdering-black-and-brown-students/2019/05.

No matter their intentions, this is the impact.
Soul-wounding, which is a deeper trauma than can be fully conveyed, impacts the part of us connected to both our divinity and humanity.

Multi-faith

We are a multi-faith family. When I explained to a dear friend that although I am a person of faith, I no longer ascribe to organized religion, she remarked: "You are like me, an unmosqued Muslim." We chuckled together with mutual understanding. Though I was raised Bahá'í, my mother held on to a particular set of Hindu beliefs steadfastly. Religion was a source of contention more than harmony. When we married, my beloved worshipped with Sufis though his parents were Methodists. Our relatives are of no faith and many faiths. The language of Bahá'í prayers & holy writings is imprinted deeply into my being. This faith is the spiritual source of my lifelong commitment to social justice & well-being. Even so, like many faith or spiritual communities, these spaces are often where our soul wounds are opened rather than healed.
We are, indeed, a multi-faith family increasingly unbelonging to our religious communities of origin.

No denialism

We wake daily to news of new violence against Black folks. Deportations are regular in the news cycle. School shootings are often old news. Those with privilege act surprised or feign shock that america is like this. Others flat-out deny it & tell us "this is not who we are." If we pay attention, we can tell the truth—that this story is over 400 years old. Black folks are policed & harmed everywhere. From traffic stops to coffee shops to the corner store to schools to streets, can Black folks go outside or drive or watch birds or sip their coffee in peace? If this is true for them, as the story of Indigenous land theft & genocide is ongoing, then how can anyone be shocked when countless forms of hate proliferate?

Stepmother

I am a stepmother. In all the cultures I have been socialized in, this identity is rarely positive. We are assumed to be evil. I brave these tropes as I create new ways to be a parent to the children of my heart & their children, too. Thank heavens, I learned that kinship is forged by motho among batho.

Together family | खानदान

Realizing that dunya looks down upon my interracial family, I have done my utmost to guard my family tenderly. I rarely share pictures of the youth or our family outside our trusted circle.
Log are likely to call our pictures beautiful, but how rarely do they truly see us in our fullness?[43]
Interracial marriages & mixed race children are not proof that racism is over. I often wonder when we will see & understand the depths of care & intention required to be in a family across races. Many of us fall apart from the relentless fractures & oppressions.

---

43. Reference to a distinctly desi expression: log kya kahenge—what will people say?

Mother of Black children

Tamir Rice would have celebrated another birthday.
Antwon Rose at seventeen was laid to rest on this day.
Black lives extinguished
eliminated by a racist system built
on committing the erasure
& purging
of Black & Indigenous people &
people of color.
Where is the freedom?
To live? To breathe? To BE?
Last week, we marked Juneteenth.
150 years of freedom
for Black folks.
Do we celebrate emancipation while
we face annihilation?
I birthed a child
fifteen years ago & named him Freedom.
I beseeched the heavens for a name
befitting a Black brown child born in america. Freedom!
Azad.
"Where is the freedom?" cry
the mothers of all the
Black Indigenous children of color.
How on earth do we birth and raise free children in a
world hell bent on extinguishing
their life force?
On this day,
I embrace all the Mothers
mourning our children's stolen lives as we pray that
one day freedom comes.

Does america love Black people?

I ask my beloved after he reflects on his father's passing from lung cancer all too soon. He was a veteran twice over who loved his country enough to go to two wars for it. I ask if america loved him when he worked at the post office or sought treatment for his cancer. My beloved and I muse that america loves Black culture and Black icons. america loves the Obamas and Oprah. america loves the exceptions & the exceptional. america loves to consume Blackness, but does this mean that america loves Black people?

Anti-Blackness energies

Do we pay attention to where & how anti-Blackness happens? It is systemic. It is not just in insults or the couched comments, but also in the energy we radiate, the way we do or do not align our intentions to ensure the safety of our Black kin. How do we listen to them? How do we pay attention to them? How do we silence them or hush them or look the other way? Whose comfort are we committed to preserving? In the answers to these questions, we can vibe anti-Blackness or solidarity.

As an american-ish
I often travel to remote
towns with my Black partner and children, now
youth,
where we enter spaces
that are not open to us.
As we receive stares and glares for
how we dare
enter here,
I know that my survival depends
upon smiling in the face of white
rage and fear.

To be american-ish
is to testify that this land
where you reside
though built on settler colonial genocide
presumes all non-white others
are infringing upon white places and white spaces, with
no accountability
for the history of settler colonial genocide that
bestowed them with this sense of entitlement.
As an american-ish,
people guess I have an accent before I even open my mouth.
As I have perfected my americanisms,
I am often met with raised eyebrows & "How
come you speak without an accent?"
As an
american-ish,
I am often compelled
to do the heavy lifting labor
of educating folks
who are white
or white-adjacent
& explaining that color blindness is a lethal form of racism.

Truthful reckoning

This is a truth that I need to contend with: we, the othered, are guilty of self-othering to meet the white gaze.
When I realize this,
I refuse to self-exoticize.
Whiteness is addicted to consuming the pain & trauma of brown others. It feeds off our grief & mourning.
I refuse to be used to satisfy the insatiable appetite for our pain.
I often refuse access to my trauma.
Instead, I offer myself as evidence of our resilience.

Let us reveal & talk about our anti-Blackness, a piece of the oppressor planted in us.

Let us consider some of the fraught discussions we brown folks must have. Those of us who are brown & american are likely to have learned our way through the maze of this place by proximity to whiteness resulting in willful anti-Blackness.

We may be brown or desi or south asian but do we behave like people of whiteness?

When I correct skinfolks on the subtle & blatant ways our anti-Blackness shows up, I am often met with a range of reactions from defensiveness or discomfort to unfriending.

Some people describe these behaviors as fragility or gaslighting or reinforcement of privilege. It is all violence.

Oppressive behaviors we display

Does brown fragility happen?

I live in the united states in the 2020s. In these times when Black Lives Matter is a globally understood movement for racial justice, we brown folks are often complicit & fall short of true allyship. We are rarely comrades. I often initiate conversations about race & anti-racism with our kin. Most often, I am greeted by the silencing techniques of "chup kar." At other times, especially with those who enjoy white-adjacent privilege, I encounter the classic playlist known as fragility: denial, gaslighting, accusation, doubling down, debating & other ways of derailing a conversation about the truth–that we are guilty of anti-Black beliefs & behaviors. Scholars debate the veracity of white fragility.[44] In lived experience, as I name these behaviors, I suspect that so-called fragility is something we desis have learned

---

44. Robin DiAngelo and Amy Landon, *White Fragility: Why It's so Hard for White People to Talk About Racism* (Beacon Press, 2018).

from the colonizers & mastered just as well as our spelling.
Non-Black folks are so immersed in anti-Blackness that we begin to display the same kind of guilt-ridden defensiveness, inaction & fragility as white folks.
Brown fragility happens. Fragility is too misleading a word for this behavior.
We cannot unlearn our anti-Blackness unless & until we heal from internalized colonialism & decolonize.

How do we react when confronted with our oppressive behaviors?

complicit silence, callous indifference, pity, denial, guilt or shame.

When presented with ideas that cause dissonance or offense, we are taught to react or overreact.

What if we respond by reflecting instead of reacting in defense?

What is the karma of brown folk[45] in settler colonialism?

Bury the model minority myth.
Refuse to be a weapon against Black america.
Refuse to erase Indigenous truths.
Refuse to ally with white supremacy.
Pay the price of refusal.

---

45. Vijay Prashad, *The Karma of Brown Folk* (University of Minnesota Press, 2001).

Stop the bakwaas | बकवास बंद करो

Black Indians exist.
Black children with desi mothers who proudly identify
as Black do exist.
Erasure of identity and brown-washing of Blackness are forms
of anti-Blackness.
We cannot demand any performance of singular identity
or affiliation from them.
Identity policing is violent.
Biracial and multiracial identifications exist.
Erasure is a form of racism.
Stop this bakwaas.
Solidarity with our biracial kin requires that we pause and consider
how our experiences both intersect and differ.

*Forcing multi-identified folks to choose only one identity is often
how white supremacy operates in identity policing.
To be desi-ish african-ish american-ish is to
revere your own mythic goddesses while you
offer deep bows to the
humans
who are rarely respected by desis.
To be american-ish desi-ish
is to call out our (not so) secret biases &
prejudices.
When the desis in america
wish silent complicity,
I speak out.
To be desi-ish & american-ish
is to refuse to make excuses for your kin who
uphold anti-Black oppressions when we
ought to dismantle the systems that oppress
us all.*

In my american-ish
existence,
I am often questioned & asked
why I affiliate consistently with Black folks.
It is implied that this is a form of reverse racism.
To be me
is to understand the unspoken
that immigrants often adapt
to white-adjacent forms of success.
I chose to align myself with my lived truths.
I decided to be an immigrant who says out loud Black
Lives Matter.
Interrupting dominant whiteness is a strategy for anti-
oppression.

Brown privilege

We hold privilege even in a world where we are stereotyped and oppressed.
When the world is proclaiming that Black Lives Matter, what is our role?
It is not our role to center ourselves and add harm to Black folks.

Who are we if we are not true in our support for Black humanity?
Who are we when we selectively claim the identity of "person of color" even as we persist in our anti-Blackness?
We have some reckoning to do with our brown privilege.
Brown accountability requires honesty.

There is a way. To center our margins.
There are ways that we can take a seat.
Be quiet, learn & make room for Black & Indigenous folks.

An opportunity comes to me. I ask myself, do I take space or make space?

When I decline & tell the person inviting me that instead of taking space, I'd like to nominate a phenomenal younger Black woman, he is flabbergasted.

Why?

He's never met a non-Black African who did this. Fellow brown folks, we have a lot of work to do. Let us make space instead of hoarding it.

Our silence & silencing of other marginalized folks is often how we perpetuate white supremacy. If we are folks of color staying silent about racism or Islamophobia or transphobia or any oppression in our midst, we uphold the here & now.

We are complicit.

I said it out loud. I put it on paper.
White supremacy uses us brown folks as tools to perpetuate itself.

When will we do our part to dismantle white supremacy?

I know we were taught to be nervous about words like this & skittish about allegations of racism. I say that it is time to use these words openly.

Defending whiteness

Let us say someone who performs allyship messes up. Hypothetically, they might be a famous or well-resourced person who garners news headlines for racist actions. What if they dress up in brownface for a party? What if they use a racist slur? Whose side do we take? Do we excuse or do we stand up for ourselves?

We might attack our skinfolk to defend a privileged white person who isn't as "for brown people" as he claims to be. Do we tell the truth? He is fundamentally a white racist. Or, do we hold them as an exception?
Exceptionalism, like tokenism, is dangerous racism.
It masquerades as one thing while it stings like another.
Let us learn that attacking each other is enacting the colonizer mentality ingrained in us.
We cannot.
Most importantly, watch how quickly we degenerate into anti-Blackness over any discourse like this because we have been slipping & sliding & refusing to believe our Black kin who warned us not to align with whiteness.
Black people have been telling us & we don't heed their warnings.
It's time for brown folks to stop erasing ourselves to uphold the status quo.
We cosign harm when we stand by in silence.

We are taught to repeat cycles of oppressions.

Hurt people hurt people

It would sadden me if you concluded that desis are exclusively harmful. I tell the truth as I have witnessed it. I do this to lay bare my heart wounds & be held accountable for ways we all harm.
It is said, hurt people hurt people. Do the oppressed oppress, too?
We do. Healing people heal people, too.

Disrupting harm

What might it look like for brown desi folks to be disruptors? What if instead of rushing to defend ourselves—saying not all of us are harmful or not all of us are anti-Black—we own up to all the ways we hold up the systems & behaviors of anti-Blackness? What if we chose to disrupt them?

We are taught to minimize or misunderstand racism.

Race lighting

Racism is violent.
It is not merely fragile privilege.
It is not an unintentional mistake.
It is often not micro.
It is not a harmless comment.
It is systemic. It is structural. It is personal.
It is violent. It is unjust.
Misnaming or minimizing racism is a form of racial gaslighting.

Rules of engagement

There is a deeply felt violence known as disowning that traumatizes many of us who venture outside desi heteronormative & casteist rules of marriage.
We come to know intimately what unbelonging means.
We are shunned & held up as examples to deter others from following suit. Even in diaspora, where interracial marriage is often accepted, desi folks rarely marry outside their race or caste, and those who do often marry white partners. There are too many hushed rules of engagement & far too many traumatic consequences as deterrents.
It is also true that interracial marriage is not proof that we are not racist.

Desi misogynoir

Brown people who watch tennis and have commentary, here are a few words I wish to convey:
We need to unlearn misogynistic anti-Blackness.
If we find ourselves describing Serena's behavior as a "tantrum" or policing her behaviors or tone by saying she was "rude" or "unprofessional" or accuse her of poor sportsmanship,
If we find ourselves commenting on her actions without understanding that what occurred is systemic, deliberate & absolutely unjust.
Let us unpack "misogynoir." This is the word Moya Bailey[46] coined to describe the specific way racism and misogyny combine to oppress Black women.

When was the last time I described desi relatives & spouses the way I describe Black women?
When was the last time I defied the patriarchy implicit in my upbringing?
When have I stood up for myself when a man did me wrong? In public? On a global stage?
Yaar, take a look in the mirror.

We see an instance of a wronged Black woman standing up for herself and take it out of the context of her daily struggles
& the relentless racism & sexism she encounters
every day everywhere.

We call her names & vilify her
when we ought to advocate for & venerate her.
If we find ourselves aligning with whiteness or defending the status-quo, if we find ourselves tone policing or otherwise replicating harmful
commentary that adds to the systemic harm to Black women & trans folks everywhere—
Stop this Misogynoir.

---

46. Moya Z. Bailey, "More on the Origin of Misogynoir," Moyazb, April 27, 2014, moyazb.tumblr.com/post/84048113369/more-on-the-origin-of- misogynoir.

Assimilation

Here is how I explain it:
Assimilating is to clap to the rhythm of those around us.
Resisting assimilation is to "clap back" with our own beat.
I resist assimilation with every clap back.

Humanity of Black folks

If we aim to shift the tides, we unlearn our bakwaas & relearn ways to engage with Black folks.
What does it mean to dignify our kin?[47]
Sometimes, deifying & putting Black folks on pedestals robs them of their humanity.
I hear my kin warn against this kind of tokenizing & I seek for ways to offer respect to those whom racism robs of humanity. They show me that it is not their job to teach me. Even as they are harmed by oppression, they are often expected to save us from our own ignorance.
This life of expectation & the tropes of "strong Black people" have exhausted or harmed them. They say again & again: we are so tired. Save the saviorism.

How can we dignify humanity?

What is our sacred responsibility for reciprocity?

---

47. Austin Channing Brown, *I'm Still Here: Black Dignity in a World Made for Whiteness* (Convergent Books, 2018).

Colonial mindset

Many of us were taught that rationality precludes emotionality.
Binary thinking is a feature of our colonized mindsets.
Unlearning binaries
reveals deep truthful insightful realities.

Caping & gatekeeping for white supremacy

The truth is that non-Black folks like me cape for white supremacy.[48]
We protect white innocence.
We are white-adjacent.
We are agents of white supremacy.
Whether in our workplaces or
hidden spaces,
do we keep gates with whiteness or
open doors for Black folks & skin folks?
We do the work of white supremacy.

Life in diaspora entails fixating on markers of identities.
It is true that our cultures &
practices are appropriated often.
As we struggle with our identities being whitewashed,
we struggle to hold on to markers of our identities
(like chai & yoga).
We enter diaspora
wars over ownership of the mundane instead of organizing
against the forces that
appropriate or extract our identities for profit.

---

48. My reflection/response to Danielle Slaughter's 2018 blog post, "All The Supremacists Are White, All of The Patriarchy Are Men, But You're Probably A Gatekeeper."

No chai

I'm a desi who rarely drinks chai.
Chai tastes of patriarchy to me.
Chai tastes of colonialism to me.
Do we imbibe high tea?
Drink it like the British or French?
Raise our pinkies & tickle our fancies?
I reject the colonial appropriations of chai.
A therapeutic desi ritual is now bereft.
I find no joy in chai.
I serve it to guests & leave my cup empty.

Chai tastes of patriarchy to me.
All the times I was commanded, "Beti, chai lao" or "chai pilao"
have made me bitter towards tea.

I wish I could've said "nah."
"Make the chai your own damn self.
You didn't birth me so I could be your personal chai-on-demand maker.
Ask my bhai to make you chai."

The one time I refused the request, I learned to swallow my defiance
& make tea in compliance.
Chai tastes of patriarchy to me.

And now when a gori barista serves up whitewashed milky froth
as chai,
I gag.
This is what cultural appropriation tastes like.
I choose black coffee, though bitter.
It tastes of defiance to me.
My occasional chai is a very bittersweet indulgence.

Chai tea activism

I hear the outcry of young brown folks calling
out the appropriation of tea
but they rarely speak up to defend Black humanity.
I wonder if there isn't a theatricality to
our duplicitous chai tea activism.

i/we

It is a function of americanism to teach us to vacillate & oscillate

between remembering "I"   & forgetting WE.

So much pendulum-like back   & forth we do

that we remember only   & rarely question the systems
individual feelings   that cause unfeelings
(victimization, oppression,   (racism, (hetero) sexism,
marginalization)   capitalism).

What if the marginalized did not marginalize?

What if we did not bleed our wounds of unbelonging all over each other? What if the wounds & scars we know did not turn into weaponized oppressive behaviors? What if we honored our moral obligation to heal fully?

Karma reckoning | कर्म

Internalized oppression is real.
Internalized oppression is really real.
Internalized oppression is really oppressive.

Cultural humility | ਨਿਮਰਤਾ

What might it mean to practice cultural humility towards Black folks?[49]
At home in Gaborone, cultural humility would mean declining the oppressive practices, taught by colonizers, of treating all Black Africans as "servants." When brown & white Africans act like the bosses of all Black folks, a part of me screams out loud about this humiliation. Where is the humility towards the keepers of this land we inhabit? At home in Decatur, sacred lands of the Muscogee Creek, cultural humility would mean learning the true history of america.

Cultural humility would mean that we non-Black folks unlearn the colonizer ways of divide & conquer. We would refuse to be model minorities who benefit from the subjugation of Black folks.

Cultural humility would mean that we do not take space. Cultural humility means that we unlearn the white-adjacent ways we have adopted.
Cultural humility invites us to relearn how to center the stories & narratives & histories of folks who built this land with unfathomable resourcefulness despite enslavement and ongoing systemic injustice.

Cultural humility means to abstain from employing the catchall category "people of color" selectively in ways that erase Black folks.

Cultural humility opens doors instead of gatekeeping.

---

49. Cynthia Foronda, et al., "Cultural Humility: A Concept Analysis," Journal of Transcultural Nursing 27, no. 3, (2016): 210–217, doi:10.1177/1043659615592677.

Cultural humility is to own up to ways we are complicit in the erasure of & systemic violence towards Black lives. Cultural humility requires that we refuse to be color-blind.

Cultural humility is to know without a shadow of a doubt that we can never fully know what it means to be raced Black in america.

Cultural humility is to honor and compensate the labor of Black folks.

Cultural humility is to see that there are as many ways to be Black as there are stars in the night sky.

Cultural humility makes way for us to be actively antiracist instead of passively non-racist.

In essence, cultural humility is akin to a deep spiritual practice in which we, non-Black folks, recenter the humanity, resilience & power of Black folks. It is a stance of opening ourselves to learning, unlearning & relearning.

Cultural humility is a prerequisite to solidarity.

Words to signal dominant (white) gaze

Exotic, ethnic, traditional, tribal,
non-white, non-English, different,
diversity,
minority.
Under-represented.
i am not interested in being compared to normative dominance or met
with representation or inclusion into whiteness.
i now refuse to other myself this way.

Nazar | نظر | नज़र

I refuse white gaze.
Refusal of white gaze will cost us.
It will also free us.

Non-white

We, the non-whites, are measured by whiteness
even as we are excluded from it.
We are taught to call ourselves everything,
even negated versions of whiteness,
but, we are expected to center & cater
to white feelings & comforts.
When we address folks as "dear white people,"
the response is defense,
even worse, but not remorse.
Whiteness does not wish to be addressed as white.
Whiteness only seeks to police who is non-white.
Even if we address whiteness,
we fear causing offense.
We might comply,
even seek adjacence.
So, how are we non-white?
Make it make sense.

DEI matters

These mistruths are often told
all over america—
"representation matters."
"diversity matters."
We are expected to accept tokenization & misrepresentation
into whiteness.
We are conditioned to seek inclusion into whiteness.
We are programmed to confuse equity into whiteness for freedom.
When everything is by default centering whiteness,
How do representation or diversity matter
when they uphold white supremacy?

Refusal

What does refusal to align with whiteness culture look like?
For me, it is to say nah to all the ways that my culture, identity &
spirit are consumed.
I do not consent to my own consumption.
Refusal feels like unbelonging,
But it is freeing.

No to cultural appropriation

How I break it down with a ten-year-old:
When in doubt, do not.
No. If your ancestors are white colonizers, know it's a big no to you.
Do not consume.
No. Sacred items aren't costumes.
No. We can't just wear things from cultures we haven't studied or
learned about.

No. We can't wear or use Indigenous items even if your great-grandfather had a First Nations parent.
No. If it's "just dress up" & superficial, it's not for us. Do not sell what's not ours.
No. We can't profit from cultural arts or practices of marginalized peoples. Do not assume.
No. Stop & think it through.
No. Even if we are people of color, we can't just take or wear or practice without learning first.
No. It's not a free-for-all.
No. If we have a shadow of a doubt, assume we cannot.

Yes, be mindful.
Yes, we can learn about our own heritages & learn to be proud of them.
Yes, we practice cultural appreciation by learning from each other.
Yes, we partake in cultural exchanges when we are invited.
Yes, we are one human family.
Yes, we are distinct cultures & peoples. Yes, be culturally humble.

Do not ever take what's not offered to you.

When in doubt, do not.

Dear white people, nah.
I rarely, if ever, address those who are white,
& if or when I might,
it is to say nah.
I refuse.

Nah to white yoga

I break out in hives when I enter
white studio spaces
where whiteness has stolen my
ancestral practices
whitewashed them
& sold them back to me diluted & poisoned with
privilege
entitlement
& callousness.
I am the brown desi-ish who
will no longer stand by as
westerners appropriate my
ancestral inheritance
& claim to "Nama-slay"
while sipping beer
doing poses in breweries sometimes
with cats and goats.
This is not yoga.
I say Nah-mastay.
Nah, you may not use or appropriate my ancestral ways.

Nah to white feminism | नही

I used to study feminism. I used to teach feminisms. In this field of study, I learned that white feminism protects whiteness. It does not uplift brown, Indigenous & Black folks. If white feminism gatekeeps for white supremacy, it is not feminism at all. The womanism of Black feminists liberates all of humanity. When Black folks are free, we are all free.[50]
I say nah to white feminism.

---

50. Combahee River Collective, "Combahee River Collective: A Black Feminist Statement," Off Our Backs 9, no. 6 (1979): 6–8, http://www.jstor.org/stable/25792966.

Gayatri Sethi

Nah to imposterism

If the yardstick to measure your worth[51] is
cisheteronormative and white,
but you are oh so "other" . . .

If the standards of success are set by white supremacy . . .
If your intelligence is measured in relation
to whiteness or
maleness
or cis-genderedness . . .

If you step back and see that
the rules,
meters
& metrics that you're measuring yourself by are all inventions for
oppression . . .

You ask for an inch tape and say nay to the yardstick
designed to keep you doubting & second-guessing yourself.

These measures are invented to demean and depress you.

Let us tell this truth:
you ain't no imposter!

You got a syndrome for real, though. It is
called oppression.
Next time you feel like an imposter, ask
yourself if it's not oppression.

You are so much more than enough.

Reframe:

The systems of oppression & exclusion are the ultimate imposters.

---

51. W. E. B. Du Bois, *The Souls of Black Folk: Essays and Sketches* (A. G. McClurg, 1903, Johnson Reprint Corp, 1968), 3.

Nah to master's tools[52]

Perfection is a master's tool.

Who taught me perfection?

Who expected my perfection?
Comparison is a master's tool.

Who compares me to whom?

Criticism is a master's tool.

Who critiques me, but not those in
power?
Conflict avoidance is a master's tool.
Silence is a master's tool.
Whose peace is kept in silence & whose
liberation is avoided?
What other master's tools make us tools,
too?

No reverse racism

Am I reverse racist because
I have committed to an
anti-racist life?
Am I reverse racist because
I seek to center
Black and Indigenous and marginalized lives?

Reverse racism is a figment of the white imagination that sees in a
disavowal from white gaze & approval an abrogation, not a liberation.
When we decolonize, we center the margins.
In america, this means we center Black & Indigenous folks.

---

52. Lorde, "Master's Tools."

Unbelonging is a weighted blanket

It weighs me down with keen awareness of my ghabrahats & heartbreaks. In its coziness, I inhale a sense of collectedness. I inhale the scents of nag champa & sage intermingled with lavender & exhale my distresses.
Unbelonging is a place of comfortable unease.
Unbelonging is a weighted blanket of cozy malaise.
I am embraced by understanding in my unbelonging.

Dismantling is unbelonging

Those who refuse to cower or center the comfort of those in power must become comfortable being villainized, removed & disdained. Dismantling systemic oppression is a commitment to unbelonging.
Is it possible that the need to belong & the policing of belonging are forms of internalized oppression?
Could it be that a path to being free is rooting in our own heritage even as we get free from belonging?

Speak belonging

I do not live belonging.
I speak the languages of belonging.
What is the lexicon of belonging?
It is the language of justice.
I have spoken & written & woven & embroidered these words into every page of this book.

Intersections

Patricia Hill Collins explains, "Intersectional paradigms remind us that oppression cannot be reduced to one fundamental type, and that oppressions work together in producing injustice."[53]

All the intersections in me are tired
I am
a brown desi-ish
considered (South Asian) though by
passport citizenship, African.

I am multifaith, not Hindu,
raised Bahá'í , presumed Muslim.

I hold extensive educational privilege with
no access to generational wealth barely
paying the bills
despite elite educational training
with debt to prove it.

I am first-generation African-born immigrant
settler to the united states married to a
descendant of the enslaved who built this land
and parent to multiracial polycultural children.

Even in the communities where I reside or
supposedly belong,
I live on the margins.
I am never the center.

Intersectionality
is as much about identity as power.

Those of us living in the intersectional margins,
who are rarely the center,
do not hold much power.

Where the intersections are so many,
we could either break open the sections &
become wholly human
or be fractured along these lines.

Let me just confess that life
in this divided world
means that all the intersections in me are tired.

& by some unfathomable means, I persist.

Herein lies my vulnerability & power.

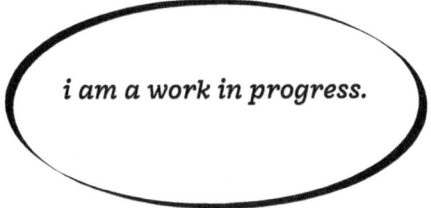

i am a work in progress.

Diasporic grief

Get over it already.
Move on. Chin up.
Grief does not have a timeline or a deadline.
We are ever in recovery.

We are ever healing
from untold losses
hopes dashed careers
derailed

---

53. Patricia Hill Collins, Black Feminist Thought: Knowledge, Consciousness, and the Politics of Empowerment (Routledge, 2000), 18, doi:https://uniteyouthdublin.files.wordpress.com/2015/01/black-feminist-though-by-patricia-hill-collins.pdf.

friends unfriended
truths silenced
possibilities dimmed
dreams dashed
plans unraveled
paths blocked
visas and permits revoked
loved ones estranged
beloveds dismayed
returns home delayed.

Grief of surviving in diaspora
is ongoing seems never ending.
Shall we maintain our facades as
unfeeling automatons tread on
march onward
unfelt and unfeeling?

Survival in diaspora?
Day to day living
requires emotional truthfulness.
This I confess–
life's grief is so real.
Its weight does some of us in.
We might succumb to it.
Grief does not have a deadline or a timeline.
We can take all the time we need to
feel.
To heal.

Freeing our emotions

If systems & structures continue to oppress us, it is also true that there are psychological & emotional wounds we bear. Many of us are deeply traumatized even as we cope & survive. If colonialism persists in the mind & on the consciousness level even as folks all over the world fight for sovereignty over their sacred lands, then decolonization must occur on an emotional & spiritual level, too. What might it feel like to heal?

Emotional processing

I cannot describe my life circumstances in detailed instances with the finesse of essayists I admire. Trauma memories have dissolved. Words often fail me. Therapy might resurrect a few realizations. There are far too many silences. That which I have not processed or healed cannot yet be spoken.
I write for emotional processing.
I gesture to events & occurrences, spaces & places, wounds & scars, realizations & inquisitions.
My unbelonging is ongoing emotional processing.

Diasporic me

Have you ever tried to explain to
your mother
in her mother tongue the
word diaspora?
Eh diaspora ki he?
What are the words
in any tongue to convey that

diasporic me
is -ish everything
& indigenous nothing?
How do I say
in my Mother's Tongue
that I do not have the words to
explain this kind
of othering
that means that belonging is always &
everywhere.
Unbelonging?
I, the speaker of many tongues, do
not have words for any of this to
identify that to live in the margins
wherever I be,
is to be in a place rich
with possibility where I
invent words & worlds
that may not yet be

To convey that I no longer seek to belong.

Gayatri Sethi

The spaces where we belong do not exist.
We build them
with radical love &
revolutionary
liberation

Notes

Reflection Invitation:

What are your working definitions of and connections between the following terms or concepts?

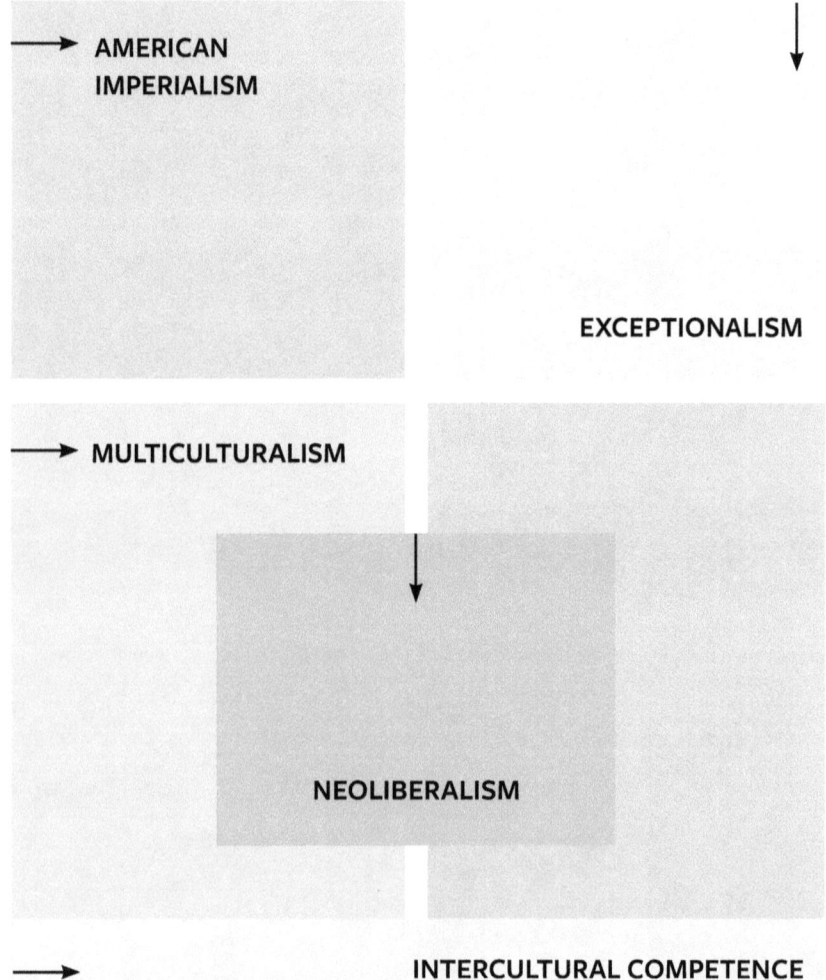

- AMERICAN IMPERIALISM
- EXCEPTIONALISM
- MULTICULTURALISM
- NEOLIBERALISM
- INTERCULTURAL COMPETENCE

```
                    PYRAMID OF WHITE SUPREMACY
                    OVERT WHITE SUPREMACY
                    COVERT WHITE SUPREMACY
                    WHITE SUPREMACY CULTURE

                    OPPRESSION SYSTEMS:
                 WHITE SUPREMACY, PATRIARCHY,
                      CASTE & CAPITALISM
```

→ **FASCISM**   **ICEBERG OF** ←
                                 CULTURE MODEL

↑ **GLOBALIZATION**

⟶ **INSTITUTIONS:** HEALTHCARE, EDUCATION, RELIGION, OR LAW ENFORCEMENT

⟶ **RACISM**
INTERNALIZED
INTERPERSONAL
STRUCTURAL
INSTITUTIONAL

PHOBIAS:
XENOPHOBIA OR
ISLAMOPHOBIA

⟶ **FORMS OF DECOLONIZATION**

Gayatri Sethi

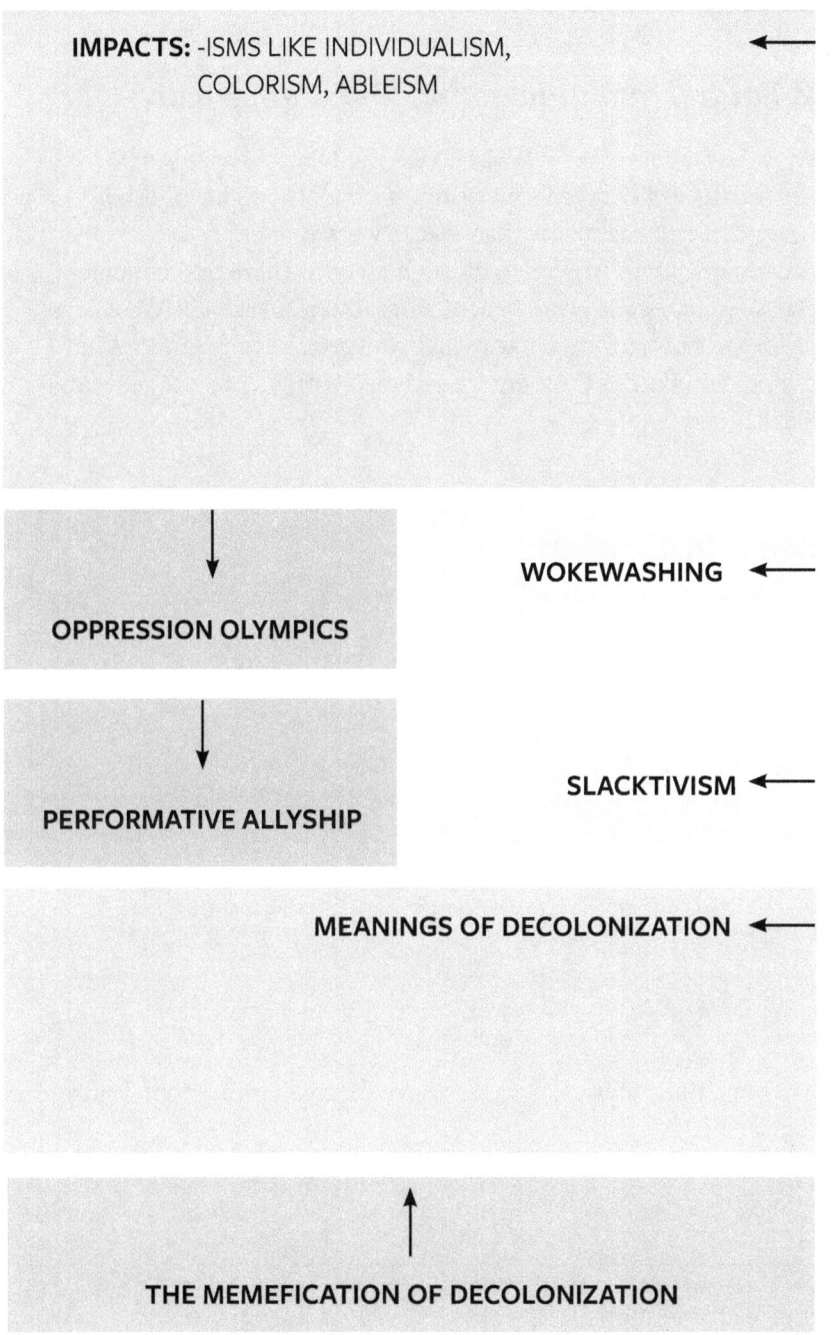

Inquiries

What are you unlearning about america?

W. E. B. Dubois asked, "What do we want? . . . We want to be Americans, full-fledged Americans, with all the rights of other American citizens. But is that all? Do we want simply to be Americans? Once in a while through all of us there flashes some clairvoyance, some clear idea, of what America really is. We who are dark can see America in a way that white Americans cannot. And seeing our country thus, are we satisfied with its present goals and ideals?[54]

What new truths will you be reckoning with about living in diaspora?

⟹

Mariame Kaba tells us, "Let this radicalize you rather than lead you to despair."[55]

---

54. W. E. B. Du Bois, "Criteria of Negro Art," The Crisis, Vol. 32 (1926), http://www.webdubois.org/dbCriteriaNArt.html.

55. Mariame Kaba, *Let This Radicalize You: Organizing and the Revolution of Reciprocal Care* (Haymarket Books, 2023).

How might accepting unbelonging offer new possibilities?

Fatima Asghar assures us,
"My people my people I can't be lost
When I see you my compass
Is brown & gold & blood"[56]

What and who define diaspora?

"What else is possible?"—Abolitionist inquiry

---

56. Asghar, "If They Should..."

SOLIDARITIES

DIASPORA·ISH

Unmake this world

This world,
so unfree, so unjust,
replete, complete was built
for our unbelonging
by empire's design.
Let there be no belonging
to empire—
it must be unbuilt,
there is only unmaking
this   world.

Unlearning and Learning

Unlearning is heart work

As much as we are taught that the work of learning is mind work, learning encompasses heart, head, and hands.
Changing our minds about something we believe to be true is heavy lifting. Imagine how much effort it requires to shift our heart feelings about a matter. Even more effort needs to be exerted to lift our hands to align with our new mindset, or moved heart set.
When our minds, hearts, and hands align, this is what it is means to work in integrity.

We must be willing to release identity and safety of belonging.

Question identity & belonging

James Baldwin explained, "Any real change implies the breakup of the world as one has always known it, the loss of all that gave one an identity, the end of safety."[57]

Identities matter, but not always in the ways we are taught they do. Belonging is a core human need, but so much harm transpires under the guise of belonging.
We are taught to lean into identity or find safety in belonging instead of reaching for something else entirely.
We mistake representation into the norm as a sign of progress instead of questioning these norms.
We might need to trade in quests for identities & belongings for new inquiries:
What do we do with our identities & belongings?
How do we make braver & safer spaces for each other?

---

57. James Baldwin, *Nobody Knows My Name* (Vintage; Reissue edition, 1992), 149.

Identities & belongings matter little unless we are leveraging these identities & belongings to welcome & value each other.

Why do identities matter if we accept unbelonging?
How do identities matter if we accept unbelonging?
What matters more than identity or belonging?

Living in diaspora is often about being perpetually maladjusted to the norms & ways of being.

Maladjusted humans

The world needs those of us who refuse to adjust to injustice.
Adjusting to capitalist exploitation is not success.
Giving in to misogyny is not survival.
Repeating cycles of oppression is not liberation.
i choose to be maladjusted.[58]
Diasporic folks, multiply othered & maladjusted, often struggle to find community.

Diasporic potential

bell hooks taught that the margin is not merely a site of deprivation.[59]
It is a potential site for liberation.
The marginalized folks in diaspora, dwelling on the margins in the core of empire, are not spots of desolation.
We are potentially sites of liberation & revolution.

---

58. Martin Luther King Jr., "Creative Maladjustment," speech, Southern Methodist University, March 17, 1966, Southern Methodist University, transcript, https://www.smu.edu/news/archives/2014/mlk-at-smu-transcript-17march1966.

---

59. bell hooks, "Choosing the Margin as a Space of Radical Openness," Framework: The Journal of Cinema and Media, no. 36 (1989): 15-23, http://www.jstor.org/stable/44111660.

Unlearn oppression

Those of us who unbelong to empire, who comprehend that
we do not seek gains within empire's status quo,
we are uninterested in reform,
we wonder how to unmake this world.

>We do not seek to be the brown/Black faces of domination.

>We aspire to be unlearners of oppression.

>We wish to become learners of revolution.

Audre Lorde writes, "The true focus of revolutionary change is never merely the oppressive situations that we seek to escape, but that piece of the oppressor which is planted deep within us."[60]

> *For many of us, personal decolonization to heal the oppressor within is overdue.*

Unfollow empire

Malcolm X warned, "They switched from the old, open colonial imperialistic approach to the benevolent approach. They came up with some benevolent colonialism, philanthropic colonialism, humanitarianism, or dollarism."[61]

Us: We need to unfollow, unsubscribe & block empire.
Them: But, wait. But, vote. But, me, my life. But, democracy.
Us: Western democracy is an invention of empire.
Them: But, vote. What about civil rights?
Civil rights were hard-fought battles for freedom.

---

60. Audre Lorde, "Age, Race, Class and Sex: Women Redefining Difference," in *Sister Outsider: Essays and Speeches* (Crossing Press, 1984), 123.

---

61. Malcolm X, "Speech at Ford Auditorium," speech, Detroit, February 14, 2965, transcript, https://www.blackpast.org/african-american-history/1965-malcolm-x-speech-ford-auditorium/.

Us: Imperial agency to vote in a settler colonial state built on land theft & genocides of Indigenous peoples now stealing the human rights of millions worldwide is not freedom.
Them: You are un-patriotic.
Us: Normalize unlearning patriotism.
Join us. Unfollow, unsubscribe & block empire.
Join us & them to cancel empire.

How do I center?

I de-center dominant narratives & narrators.
                              Inch by inch, moment by moment,
                          breath by breath, I center the margins.
              I center myself & my soul.
I recenter the marginalized collective.

Learn anti-racism

I realize that by virtue of growing up on the African continent, I learned a distinct way of seeing the world that centers Black joy, resilience, beauty & glory. Blackness was normative in an expansive sense.
Even today on american soil, my children very rarely encounter this celebration of Blackness.
On my lifelong anti-racism journey, I have come to understand that my role is to continue learning, be humble & amplify the humanity of the most marginalized in its abundant forms. I do this learning in intimate & communal ways, by teaching & community building with like-hearted people.

Interrupt injustice

I am an injustice interrupter because I am well-versed in unbelonging. I often wonder how I might put my body, voice & extensive knowledge in the way of harm against my Black kin. I have a role & responsibility to be anti-racist & many of the verses that speak out & call out the -isms in my communities are intended as disruptive forms of collective care.
Is it not loving to tell the truth in the service of justice?

Make new identities

We identify by actions, not just labels or markers.

We are caretakers, caregivers, creators, knowledge makers, movement comrades, cultural workers, protestors . . .

Learn nuance

Our conflicted confounded world at
war with itself
is crying out for nuance.
We the margins we
the marginal,
we see & be all the nuances.
Let us search for nuance, let us
invent new words
& worlds.
I suggest looking at the margins.
When the margins are seen,
when the margins are heard, nuance lives.

Share power

We are taught to fear power.
We are expected to rise to power.
We might cower to those who hold power.
We often seek power over the power
less.
What if less
or more, nonetheless, we share power?

Bear witness

Bearing witness is not passive eyes on atrocity.
Bearing witness to genocides is not about empathy.
Bearing witness is an active stance to ensure dignity.

Resist dehumanization

There are a million ways to resist oppression.
Do not deny the devastation.
Do not focus only on doom, despair, danger, death & demolition.

There are a million or more dangers
lurking in sharing only
dehumanization.

There are a billion ways
to resist dehumanization.

Learn languages of liberation

One of the realities of my life here in the sacred lands of the Muscogee is that I have accrued significant cultural capital. This educational privilege means that I can speak as fluently in the words of whiteness or academia as I can in the words of my mother's tongue. Sometimes, I speak academic lingo more fluently than words of affection or care.
There is an alienation in this reality. One outcome is that it is here that I have learned the language of feminisms, critical race theories & abolition, too. I have learned to unlearn ableist language & relearn words that are more encompassing or inclusive. I have witnessed the power of words that alienate & phrases that signal sanctuary.

Aliyekupanidisha simpige teke. Do not kick the one who helped you up. Why look down on your humble origins?

Honor heritage

I realized that the more we are in touch with our heritage, the more the ancestors whisper in our hearts the truths that tie us together. I used to teach my students that learning is about activating not just the head, but also our hearts & hands.
Eventually, I realized this is a core teaching of Sikhi guiding me through my beji, dwelling deep in my core.
Seva. Tan. Man. Dhan. | ਸ"ਵਾ | तन मन धन

A love note to the marginalized maladjusted

We are not alone.

those of us who are -ish or
rarely fit in
or exist only on the margins
when survival mode reigns &
joy is so very rare,
maybe we do not belong anywhere.

Maybe home is not a place.
Maybe our trauma wounds bleed too often.

May we find comfort in knowing that we are not alone.
May we find people who embrace us.
May we be met with understanding & validation.
May we know what sanctuary feels like.
May we imagine, dream, & conjure our liberation.

This is our mantra: **We Got Us.**

Collective Dreaming

Open heart living

The world might disappoint me.
Those I care for might betray me.
People do break my heart.

Yes, I might be hurt.
Yes, an open heart can be a broken heart.
Yes, I am vulnerable this way.

I choose to be open anyway.
Love and live any way.
Broken hearts see and bleed love everywhere.

Pyar revolution

Once i learn to love myself, it is
a revolution.
Love yourself
even if nobody loves you.
My pyar encompasses my people, my batho.[62]

---

62. Batho is the Setswana word for people, or a collective. It references ubuntu.

Pyarful languages of liberation | एकता | ਏਕੀਕਰਣ

What are the pyar practices of those subjected to perpetual othering, marginalization, discrimination & policing?

Truth
Reckoning
Accountability
Reparations
Abolition
Liberation
Dignity
Humanity
Humility
Reciprocity
Community
Solidarity

Liberation praxis | آزادی | आज़ादी

humanity | मानवता | integrity | अखंडता

May other humans grant us the grace & acceptance we grant them.
May there be space & place for us all to be humanly human.

May our lives be testimony.
May integrity guide us
to be vigilant in ensuring that our thoughts,
words & deeds align truthfully & truly.

May we remember
our lives are a slippery dance.
We may trip & fall.

There are systemic traps and
personal triggers
that leave us feeling less than.

May we not make space within for feeling less than.
May we think liberating thoughts, feel freeing feelings
& work actively to ensure collective well-being.
May values & beliefs from heritage guide us to soulful authenticity.

Hopeful audacity

What does hope look like?[63]

Some days, hope is driving your children to their cello lesson.

Hope might be double masking to meet a
relative six feet apart.

Hope is interfaith kinship & chosen family bonds.

What does hope feel like?

Hope feels like a walk in the winter rain to visit
Mom's resting place on her birthday.

Like teaching.

Like writing & creating.

What does hope feel like?

---

63. This piece is inspired by Jesse Jackson, "Keep Hope Alive," (speech, Atlanta, GA, July 19, 1988), American Radio Works, https://americanradioworks.publicradio.org/features/blackspeech/jjackson.html.

Hope feels like a deep commitment to learning.

Hope jumps off my overfull bookshelves with titles by radical authors.
Hope is embodied in my children as they grow beauteous in their own skins.
Hope has an audacity to it.

Hope does not shy away from struggle.

Hope looks like struggle or protest.
Hope feels like revolution.

Abolitionist scholar, Ruha Benjamin, writes about the importance of developing visionary imagination. She advises, "We must populate our imaginations with images and stories of our shared humanity, of our interconnectedness, of our solidarity as people—a poetics of welcome, not walls."[64]

I extend this invitation to
collective decolonial dreaming.

Such collective dreaming requires collective unlearning of domination.

Decolonizing is unforgetting

Decolonizing is unforgetting the collective connections.
Decolonizing is unraveling our soul wounds of isolation in diaspora.
Decolonizing is unbreaking the trauma breaks.
Decolonizing is undoing collective indoctrinations.
Decolonizing is unmaking empire.

---

64. Ruha Benjamin, *Imagination: A Manifesto* (W. W. Norton & Company, 2024), 102.

Decolonial feminist Breny Mendoza, in the translated essay "The Undemocratic Foundations of Democracy,"[65] lays bare the extent to which what we know as democracy is a device of colonial-imperial power that began in 1492 with the colonization of the Americas.

Too many of us worldwide are indoctrinated
into confusing this form of coloniality with freedom.

Dream decolonial dreams

I envision a day
when 300 million of any currency will
be raised in under a day
by colonizers as
reparations
to restore the rightful dues of
the Indigenous and the colonized.
I more so dream of a day when 300 or more million
will be spent in under a day as restoration by
colonizers
to recreate the pillaged and stolen
    artifacts
    histories
    gifts
of the formerly colonized.
Those millions would be wiser invested in
reparations
to a future civilization than
restoration
of symbols of old.

---

65. Breny Mendoza, "The Undemocratic Foundations of Democracy: An Enunciation from Postoccidental Latin America," Signs 31, no. 4 (2006): 932–39, https://doi.org/10.1086/500607.

Border-free living

Harsha Walia tells us, "Butterflies have always had wings; people have always had legs. While history is marked by the hybridity of human societies & the desire for movement, the reality of most of migration today reveals the unequal relations between rich & poor. Between South and South, between whiteness & its others."[66]

Those of us dwelling in diaspora measure our distances to each other by visas, passports, costs of airfares
& countless months or years of separation from homelands & relations abroad.

We dream of borderless, boundary-free, diasporic third spaces capable of welcoming our humanity.

We bear witness to realities and angsts of immigrating.
We complain to each other: I hate it here.
We respond with dismay: But, where do we even go from here?

If we seek to belong to the colony too much,
we will need to conform to policy too unjust,
that harms, polices, detains, and deports folks just like us.

If we seek to be free,
we will need to unbelong to colony to imagine a world border,
passport
& duty free.

---

66. Harsha Walia, *Undoing Border Imperialism* (AK Press, 2013), 19.

Soulful sumud[67]

My dear friend asks me: how do you stay hopeful when the world is so unbearable. She is bearing the daily heaviness of living in diaspora while her peoples are enduring an ongoing Nakba and genocide.

Honestly, hope is evasive. Our tanks of endurance are empty.
We are told that we find reservoirs of hope in collectives.

Hopelessly in search of hope itself, we might persist with those who search together, too.

I half joke when I tell her that my optimism is old. I am old. I remember when our neighbors to the north were still named Rhodesia. That name is no more. That colonial occupation is no more. I recall when our neighbors to the south built apartheid regimes and walls, aggressing our borders by night, occupying our nightmares as much as our day prayers. Those walls are no more. South African Apartheid is no more. I know I am old, but I do not believe lies we are sold about the absolute power of occupying, colonizing forces. I know in my old bones that these walls will fall, and these occupations will end. I know that in every land, the people rise, they do not concede. They do not bend or surrender.

Another habibti, chosen sister, bonded with me by mutual soul-searching, often whispers the word sumud. Sumud, she says, especially on particularly trying days of relentless death and demise of her kin in Gaza. I am still learning about the true depths and meanings of collective steadfastness conjured by the word sumud.[67]

There might be no accurate way to convey that sumud seeds hopes and optimisms, like an orchard of olive trees on lands from river to sea, that have been occupied for decades, but have not as yet ceded or surrendered. I marvel at the possibilities that solidarity, whatever this means, might be seeded in soils enriched with sumud.[68]

---

67. Sumud or sumoud is an Arabic word for steadfastness or resilience. Among Palestinians, it signifies collective resistance and perseverance in the face of ongoing occupation of their homelands.

Gayatri Sethi

What kind of sumud rich harvests will we enjoy when liberation comes, together, in collectives of people rising, among feasts of olives, overlooking a free sea where we together exhale breathe, just soulfully be. May we just be soulfully free. Collectively.

Defenders of immigrant and Indigenous rights yell, "They tried to bury us, they did not know we were seeds." "Quisieron enterrarnos, pero no sabían que eramos semillas."

I write this with and for my soul siblings:

> Sumud, my siblings. Steadfastness, see?
>
> Sow seeds of sumud, siblings.
> Stay together in solidarity
>
> Soulfully.
> As the seeds sprout and spread,
> Sabr.
> Inshallah
> we see,
>
> side by side,
> soul of my soul,
>
> simultaneously,
> we shall harvest
>
> liberations
> Steadfastness, see.

---

68. This meditation is inspired by multiple conversations with Safa Suleiman, Palestinian-American educator and author. This concept is elucidated in the anthology, *Sumud: A New Palestinian Reader*, edited by Malu Halasa and Jordan Elgrably (Seven Stories Press, 2025).

Sahaara Aspirations | ਸਹਾਰਾ

I aspire to lead my life in such a way that I am a soft place to land for folks who are intimately oppressed by forces of unbelonging.
May we find each other. May we know reciprocity & mutuality. May we offer each other sahaara[69] & hosla.
May we tell brave truths to each other. May we call each other in for our bakwaas.
May we speak radical healing love into each others' broken hearts.
May we heal collectively. May our existence be a balm. May our solidarity be rooted in our virsa & extend to all humanity.[70]

>Let us conjure & imagine new worlds & possibilities.
>Let us reroot in humanity & heritage.

Aatma da kam

In order to work the world, we must rework ourselves. Many wisdom keepers across time and space have reiterated this truth.
>In Sikhi, inner soul work[71] is called aatma da kam.

This inner working is linked up with practices in service, seva, to the collective.[72]
>Aatma da kam is seva is rooted in virsa.

---

69. Sahaara is a Punjabi word for support. It is the name of a character in Jasmin Kaur's novel *If I Tell You The Truth* (Harper Collins, 2021). This verse invites reflection on Sikhi principles that inform actions.

70. Virsa is a Punjabi word for heritage.

71. Victoria Gill, "Intersectional(ity) Pedagogy: Conceptualizing Soul Work towards Solidarity and Resistance," The Educational Forum, 86 no. 4 (2022): 382–95, doi:10.1080/0 0131725.2022.210182.

72. I. K. Grewal, "Seva +: A Framework for ASLCE practice and research," International Journal of Research on Service-Learning and Community Engagement, 11 no. 1 (2023). doi.org/10.37333/001c.91722.

Solidarity ... Solidarities

Solidarity statements

As a diasporic descendant or Punjabi peoples rendered refugees by colonial violence during partition, i stand in solidarity with all oppressed peoples.

As an African-ish person raised on the continent during Apartheid, i stand in unwavering solidarity with all peoples struggling to end occupation and apartheid on their lands.

As an immigrant to the americas, i stand unequivocally with all migrants, displaced peoples & refugees in our collective efforts to dismantle border regimes while supporting land back to Indigenous peoples.

As a co-learner, i stand soulfully with all those striving to learn how to stand in solidarity with causes & peoples whose truths & rights are being unjustly violated.

As a multi-identified human, i stand in solidarity with liberation movements across identifications & belongings, with earnest respect for our mutual humanity.

Unbelonging is solidarity

Wherever I go   I am fluid   & I flow   past belonging   into Solidarity.

Is it not ironic that solid-arity   is not so solid after all?

It is flowing   awareness   consciousness   being.

I muse but I do not conclude: is solidarity possible if we are too settled in our identities?

Perhaps if we identify too deeply along rigid boundaries of race   gender   ethnicity   nationality   or are too set in our beliefs ideologies   communities,   we might not flow?

I wonder if belonging, like solidarity, calls for fluidity.

Solidarity summons

Solidarity extends & expands who is included in our us. We extend our circles & connections in ever-expanding mutual & iterative relations.

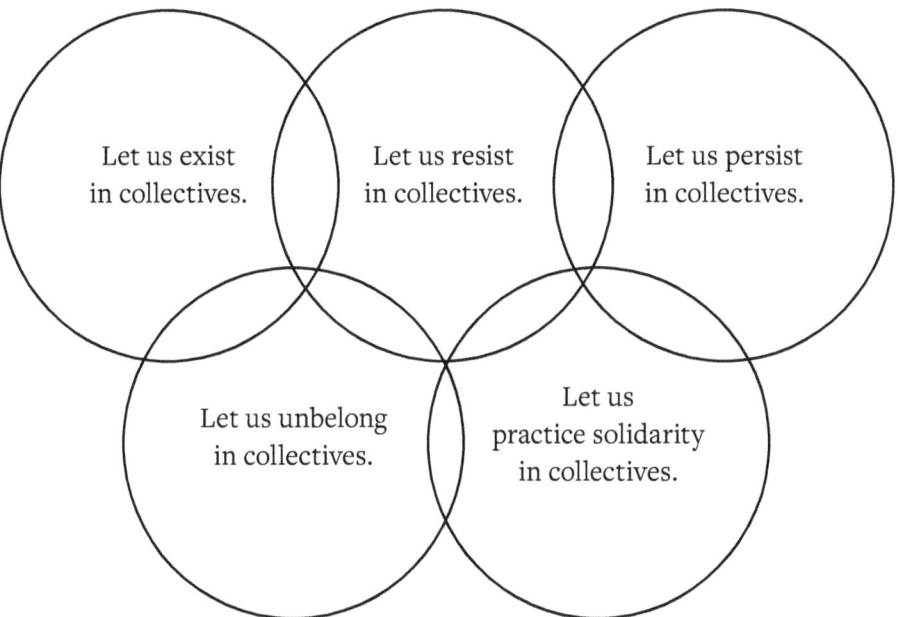

Solidarity struggles

Solidarity struggles sometimes.
Solidarity may be a struggle song,

Slow steady,
sometimes solemn.

Solidarity is a sound wave
breaking through
 barriers
 fences
 walls
of silence
built by humans, states & empires.

Solidarity is not SILENT

As countless atrocities unfold globally to here at home,
As genocides are debated but not abated from Palestine to Congo to Sudan to Indigenous unceded lands we call home.

As the martyr death counts rise & bombs drop,
day after day after month after month,
do we look away?
Do we deny or justify?
Do we hold silences untold,
callousness manifold,
hearts cold?

Solidarity is not, cannot be silent or untold.

Solidarity stands

I stand with_____
We stand in solidarity with_____

Be disloyal to your generation.
Be anti-patriotic to your nation.
Be unbelonging to your community.
Be unwavering in your solidarity.
Solidarity necessitates willingness to defy communal norms
& constraints that discipline us into conformity.
Solidarity critiques self & systems.
Solidarity requires audacity to transgress identity & culture.

Solidarity sings

When solidarity sings, of multitudes magnifying
   soulful notes bring growing free wings. centering
     solace & sahaara   Solidarity sings the voices of the most silenced.
                         with a chorus

Revolutions

Let us reconfigure identity & belonging into revolutionary solidarity.

Toni Cade Bambara taught us, "We'd better take time to fashion revolutionary selves, revolutionary lives, revolutionary relationships. Mouth don't win the war. It don't even win the people."[73]

Liberation is heart work. Liberation is collective work. Liberation is a call to collective action.

Center the margins, comrades. Center us, not just ourselves.

---

[73]. Toni Cade Bambara, "On Roles," in *The Black Woman: An Anthology*, ed. Toni Cade Bambara (New American Library, 1970), 110.

What are you working towards?

What are you practicing?

What is your life work?

–Abolitionist inquiries

Life working

If I am honest, I work toward truth, to unlearn & learn again.
If I am being aspirational, I work for inquilab & intifada revolution.
If I am being audacious, I work for collective azadi liberation.

Do you identify as a revolutionary?

Toni Cade Bambara inspires:
"As a culture worker who belongs to
an oppressed people, my job is to
make revolution irresistible."[74]

Revolt | ਰੇਵਲੂਸ਼ਨ

The jolt to revolt
is a spark that turns into a flame to
burn down oppressive ways.

Are you attracted to revolt & rebellion?

---

74. Toni Cade Bambara, "An Interview with Toni Cade Bambara: Kay Bonetti," in *Conversations with Toni Cade Bambara*, ed. Thabiti Lewis (University Press of Mississippi, 2012), 35.

Rebellion-Revolution

"Burn it down"

Rebellion is an outside job.
Jolt to rebel sparked by an event.
Rebellion is reactive
Spurts of outbursts
Sputtering out
Until another unjust oppression.
Seemingly random, disobedient, Unruly.

Revolution is an inside job.
Jolt to revolt is ever apparent.

Revolution is active
Sustainably strategic
Slow burning
Constant even during apparent submission.
Seeming calm, peaceful harmony.

Revolt or revolution. It is not a binary, but there is a distinction.

Words for Revolution

Intifada	Inquilab	Biplaba
Thawra	Mapinduzi	Hyeogmyeong

Words for liberation

- Tahrir | تَحْرِير
- Inkululeko
- Ukombozi
- Mukti | মুক্তি
- Azadi | آزادی
- Mukati | ਮੁਕਤੀ
- Hyeokmyeong | 혁명

Frantz Fanon explains the importance of centering people: "What it means is to try, relentlessly and passionately, to teach the masses that everything depends on them; that if we stagnate it is their responsibility, and that if we go forward it is due to them too, that there is no such thing as a demiurge . . . that the demiurge is the people themselves and the magic hands are finally only the hands of the people."[75]

---

75. Frantz Fanon, *The Wretched of the Earth* (Grove Press, 1963), 197.

June Jordan told us, "We are the ones we've been waiting for."[76]

Solidarity politics

Solidarity politics among people might save us.
Peoples' movements save us.
People-centered revolutions for global solidarity will save us.

Most revolutions are about land, bread, and dignity for the people by the people.

Solidarity sayings

> The people united will never be defeated.

> In our thousands and in our millions, we are all Palestinians.

> None of us are free until all of us are free.

> Exist! Resist! Return!

> Generation after generation until total liberation.

> Inquilab zindabad!

Peoples' revolutionary movements

From Kanaki to Kenya,
Bangladesh to Congo,
Niger to Sudan,

---

76. June Jordan, "Poem for South African Women," *Passion* (Copper Canyon Press, 1980)

the people rebel
against forces of state fascism
while resisting global forces of empire.

Across state borders, the protests resonate & echo—
      "The people united will never be defeated."
We strike, we appeal, we refuse to cower to power.
Our struggles & liberations are deeply, intricately
interconnected once we see that in solidarity,
none of us are free unless all of us are free.

> "One struggle, many fronts"
>
> "There is only one solution.
> Intifada revolution"

Fight fire with fire

Fred Hampton said: "We don't think you fight fire with fire best; we think you fight fire with water best. We're going to fight racism not with racism, but we are going to fight with solidarity." [77]
They say: Do not fight fire with fire.
I reply: Our fire for liberation from oppression
is not the same fire of oppressive hate.
Our fires are not the same.
How we fight fires is not the same.
We flight the fires of oppressions
with the flows of solidarity.

---

77. Fred Hampton, "We Have to Protect Our Leaders!," speech, Capitol Theater, May 19, 1969, Marxists Internet Archive, https://www.marxists.org/archive/hampton/1969/05/19.htm.

Invocation for liberation

Liberation is a way of life.
It is not a sign in my front yard.
It is not a neat reading list.
It is not a checklist.
It is a practice.
It is a mindset & most of all, a heartset.
I vow to exert constant effort & willingness to un/learn.
As I commit to this ongoing daily work in a world where systemic & pervasive oppressions persist.

Reworking life work

Even though as a scholar and educator, I value book learning and reading for liberation, this is not enough. Growing up in southern Africa, with ubuntu practices, these words resonate deeply for me as a call to collective learning practiced with and centering people. I am still relearning the possibilities for this kind of learning.

> Revolutions are often born of struggle.
> Interconnected struggles build revolutions.

When I visited my mother in Gaborone recently, we had a tender conversation about my unconventional life path. I confessed that as much as I wanted to be an educator and professor, my struggle with oppressions forced another path for me. My mother, though disappointed that I have not found success in a conventional career path, remarked thoughtfully that I am becoming a krantikari. This is her mother tongue's word for revolutionary. I reluctantly accept her reluctant admission. She remembered that though her own mother had died tragically in partition times, had she survived, she would have been a krantikari. We nodded in silence at the recognition that revolutionary ancestors guide us. Whether we reckon with this or not, it is our work to do. Among Sikh folks, aatma da kam (soul work) is a way of conveying this inner working. None of us are exempt from this work especially if we are descended of colonized, displaced people.

This path is unclear and at times, feels untrodden.

bell hooks taught us that "your heart has to be ready to handle the weight of your calling."[78] This is why I often say that liberation is heart work. Until I grappled with teachings by Assata Shakur, Audre Lorde & bell hooks, I have not been able to reckon with what this calling might be. I am unlearning to identify as an educator or student, even. I am learning to identify as a cultural worker, knowledge worker, aspiring abolition worker.

Revolutionary work is our work to do. If we fear for our survival, if we are at a loss, wondering how to survive, we might remember:

survival is a promise,[79]
survival is revolutionary work,
survival is collective revolutionary work,
survival is a collective promise.

Revolutionary aesthetics without revolutionary actions are counter-revolutionary.

---

78. DJ Lynnée Denise, "Soulful Critical Thought: bell hooks and the Making of a DJ Scholar," DJ Lynnée Denise, n.d., http://www.djlynneedenise.com/dj-scholarship-bell-hooks.

---

79. Alexis Pauline Gumbs, *Survival Is a Promise: The Eternal Life of Audre Lorde* (Farrar, Straus and Giroux, 2024).

Notes

Reflection Invitation:

What are your working definitions of and connections between the following terms or concepts?

LIBERATION

ANTI-IMPERIALISM

RESISTANCE MOVEMENTS

ABOLITION

Inquiries

Why do we shift from learning about identity & belonging to practicing solidarity?

Angela Davis told us, "Neoliberal ideology drives us to focus on individuals, ourselves, individual victims, individual perpetrators?"[80]

What does collective liberation demand of us?

Assata Shakur tells us revolution requires sacrifice:
"are you ready to sacrifice to end world hunger. To sacrifice to end colonialism.
To end neo-colonialism. to end racism. to end sexism.
r/evolution means the end of Exploitation.
r/evolution means
Respecting people from other cultures.
r/evolution is creative . . .
r/evolution is love."[81]

What new learnings & possibilities lie in practicing solidarity?

Davis says, "It is in collective that we find reservoirs of hope and optimism."[82]

How will we revise our life working to reflect new learning?

---

80. Angela Y. Davis, *Freedom is a Constant Struggle: Ferguson, Palestine, and the Foundations of a Movement* (Haymarket, 2016), 141.

---

81. "This is the 21st century and we need to redefine r/evolution...," words attributed to Assata Shakur.

---

82. Davis, 59.

Create your own inquiries

Gayatri Sethi

Imagine a list of actions and activisms

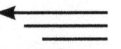

APPENDIX

Gratitudes and acknowledgements

I am beyond grateful to all the folks who have read my words and encouraged me to write this book. Because of you all, I am braver. Thanks to every reader, past and future, I have persisted in efforts to revise my first book into a new form with additional clarifications and connections.

I felt deeply guided by family, collectives, the ancestors, and kin on my writing journey.

We got us.

This book is a collaboration among numerous creatives for whom I hold deep respect. I'm thankful to Ambika Sambasivan and Suhani Parikh for investing and believing in this project. The creative finesse and loving attention of Annika Sarin's design and artistry brought life to my words. I'm thankful for Mitali's editing attentiveness. Jamila's labors of care carry all my endeavors.

My writing community and friends—too many to name—have supported me in ways I can't fully express. Some of them, gifted writers, poets, and scholars themselves, are owed special thanks: Adiba, Priyanka, Reem, Rita, Iman, Simran, Esmé, Vctoria, Neema, Ivania, Karuna, Karen, Safa, Susan, George, Navjot, Leila, Aya, and Shifa. Earnest gratitude is offered to folks who have generously provided praise and recommendations of this book. The booktok and bookstagram community who uplift educational readings are truly appreciated.

I am inspired by the ones who call me mama, bibi, aunty, and comrade. It is my hope for and faith in them that prompted me to recreate this book as an offering of community care for collective learning.

Gayatri Sethi

Some verses were previously published in

South Asian Today
Dissident Voice
Brown Girl Magazine
The Aerogram

Works cited

Adichie, Chimamanda Ngozi. "The danger of a single story." TED: Ideas Worth Spreading, July 2009, www.ted.com/talks/chimamanda_ngozi_adichie_the_danger_of_a_single_story.

Ahmed, Sara. *The Feminist Killjoy Handbook*. Penguin Books, 2024.

Ambedkar, B. R. *Annihilation of Caste: The Annotated Critical Edition*. Edited by S. Anand. Verso, 2014.

Andrews, Kehinde. "I Compared Universities to Slave Plantations to Disturb, Not Discourage." *The Guardian*. October 24, 2016. https://www.theguardian.com/commentisfree/2016/oct/24/universities-slave-plantations-racist.

Asghar, Fatima. "If They Should Come For Us." Poetry Foundation. March 2017. www.poetryfoundation.org/poetrymagazine/poems/92374/if-they- should-comefor-us.

Australian Human Rights Comission. "Lateral violence in Aboriginal and Torres Strait Islander communities." Social Justice Report 2011. https://humanrights.gov.au/our-work/publications/chapter-2-lateral-violence-aboriginal-and-torres-strait-islander-communities.

Baldwin, James. *Nobody Knows My Name*. Vintage; Reissue edition, 1992.

Bambara, Toni Cade. "On Roles." *The Black Woman: An Anthology*, edited by Toni Cade Bambara. New American Library, 1970.

Bambara, Toni Cade. "An Interview with Toni Cade Bambara: Kay Bonetti." *Conversations with Toni Cade Bambara*, edited by Thabiti Lewis. University Press of Mississippi, 2012.

Benjamin, Ruha. *Imagination: A Manifesto.* W. W. Norton & Company, 2024.

Benjamin, Ruha. "Ruha Benjamin—Spelman Convocation 2024." April 11, 2024. Posted April 16, 2024, by Outspoken Agency. YouTube, 14:55. https://www.youtube.com/watch?v=j_12_E3LAeg&ab_channel=OutspokenAgency.

Brown, Austin Channing. *I'm Still Here: Black Dignity in a World Made for Whiteness.* Convergent Books, 2018.

Collins, Patricia Hill. *Black Feminist Thought: Knowledge, Consciousness, and the Politics of Empowerment.* Routledge, 2000.

Combahee River Collective. "Combahee River Collective: A Black Feminist Statement." *Off Our Backs* 9, no. 6 (1979): 6–8.

Davis, Angela Y. *Freedom is a Constant Struggle: Ferguson, Palestine, and the Foundations of a Movement.* Haymarket, 2016.

DiAngelo, Robin and Amy Landon. *White Fragility: Why It's so Hard for White People to Talk About Racism.* Beacon Press, 2018.

DJ Lynnée Denise. "Soulful Critical Thought: bell hooks and the Making of a DJ Scholar." DJ Lynnée Denise, n.d. http://www.djlynneedenise.com/dj-scholarship-bell-hooks.

Du Bois, W. E. B. "Criteria of Negro Art." *The Crisis* 32 (1926).

Du Bois, W. E. B. *The Souls of Black Folk: Essays and Sketches.* A. G. McClurg, 1903. Johnson Reprint Corp, 1968.

Faloyin, Dipo. *Africa Is Not a Country: Notes on a Bright Continent.* W. W. Norton & Company, 2022.

Fanon, Frantz. *The Wretched of the Earth.* Grove Press, 1963.

Fanon, Frantz and Charles L. Markmann. *Black Skin, White Masks.* Grove Press, Inc., 1967.

Foronda, Cynthia, et al. "Cultural Humility: A Concept Analysis." *Journal of Transcultural Nursing.* 27 no. 3 (2016): 210–217.

Freire, Paulo. *Pedagogy of the Oppressed.* Continuum Press, 1970.

Gay, Roxane. "Roxane Gay on How to Write Trauma." Interview by Monica Lewinsky. *Vanity Fair.* February 18, 2021. https://www.vanityfair.com/style/2021/02/roxane-gay-on-how-to-write-about-trauma.

Gill, Victoria. "Intersectional(Ity) Pedagogy: Conceptualizing Soul Work toward Solidarity and Resistance." *The Educational Forum* 86 no.4 (2022): 382–95.

Grewal, I. K. "Seva +: A Framework for ASLCE practice and research." *International Journal of Research on Service-Learning and Community Engagement* 11 no.1 (2023).

Gumbs, Alexis Pauline. *Survival Is a Promise: The Eternal Life of Audre Lorde.* Farrar, Straus and Giroux, 2024.

Halasa, Malu and Jordan Elgrably, eds. *Sumud: A New Palestinian Reader.* Seven Stories Press, 2025.

Hall, Stuart with Bill Schwarz. *Familiar Stranger: A Life Between Two Islands.* Duke University Press Books, 2017.

Hampton, Fred. "We Have to Protect Our Leaders!" Speech, Capitol Theater, May 19, 1969. Marxists Internet Archive. https://www.marxists.org/archive/hampton/1969/05/19.htm.

hooks, bell. *Feminism is for Everybody: Passionate Politics.* South End Press, 2000.

hooks, bell. "Choosing the Margin as a Space of Radical Openness." *Framework: The Journal of Cinema and Media* no. 36 (1989): 15–23.

Jackson, Jesse. "Keep Hope Alive." Speech, Democratic National Convention, July 19, 1988, Omni Coliseum, Atlanta, GA. American Radio Works. americanradioworks.publicradio.org/features/blackspeech/jjackson.html

Jaleel, Muzamil. "Poetry in commotion." *The Guardian.* July 29, 2002. www.theguardian.com/world/2002/jul/29/kashmir.india.

Jordan, June. "Poem for South African Women." Poets.org. https://poets.org/poem/poem-south-african-women.

Kaba, Mariame. *Let This Radicalize You: Organizing and the Revolution of Reciprocal Care.* Haymarket Books, 2023.

Kaur, Jasmin. *If I Tell You the Truth.* Harper, 2021.

King, Martin Luther Jr. "Creative Maladjustment." Speech, Southern Methodist University, March 17, 1966. Southern Methodist University. Transcript. https://www.smu.edu/news/archives/2014/mlk-at-smu-transcript-17march1966.

Lorde, Audre. *Sister Outsider: Essays and Speeches.* Crossing Press, 1984.

Love, Bettina. "How Schools Are 'Spirit Murdering' Black and Brown Students." *Education Week.* May 24, 2019. https://www.edweek.org/leadership/opinion-how-schools-are-spirit-murdering-black-and-brown-students/2019/05.

Malhotra, Aanchal. "Partition of India: Objects that tell the story of a mass exodus." CNN Style. August 8, 2017. https://www.cnn.com/style/article/india-pakistan-partition-remnants-of-separation/index.html.

Mendoza, Breny. "The Undemocratic Foundations of Democracy: An Enunciation from Postoccidental Latin America." *Signs* 31, no. 4 (2006): 932–39.

Mock, Janet. *Redefining Realness: My Path to Womanhood, Identity, Love & So Much More*. Atria Books, 2014.

Mohanty, Chandra. "Under Western Eyes: Feminist Scholarship and Colonial Discourses." *Feminist Review* 30, no. 1 (1988): 61–88.

Moya Z. Bailey. "More on the Origin of Misogynoir." Moyazb. April 27, 2014. moyazb.tumblr.com/post/84048113369/more-on-the-origin-of- misogynoir.

Mpamira-Kaguri, Tabitha. "Trauma not Transformed is Trauma Transferred: What Baton are you passing on?" Hosted by TedxOakland. November 2019. Posted December 3, 2019, by Tedx Talks. YouTube, www.ted.com/talks/tabitha_mpamira_kaguri_trauma_not_transformed_is_trauma_transferred_what_baton_are_you_passing_on.

Prashad, Vijay. *The Karma of Brown Folk*. University of Minnesota Press, 2007.

Rodney, Walter. *How Europe Underdeveloped Africa*. Verso, 2018.

Said, Edward W. *Culture and Imperialism*. Vintage Books, 1994.

Slaughter, Danielle. "All The Supremacists Are White, All of The Patriarchy Are Men, But You're Probably A Gatekeeper." Mamademics. December 7, 2018. www.mamademics.com/supremacists-white-patriarchy-men- youre-gatekeeper/.

Spivak, Gayatri Chakravorty. "Can the Subaltern Speak?" in *Marxism and the Interpretation of Culture*, edited by Cary Nelson and Lawrence Grossberg. University of Illinois Press, 1988.

Thiong'o, Ngũgĩ wa. *Decolonising the Mind: the Politics of Language in African Literature.* James Currey, 1986.

Walia, Harsha. *Undoing Border Imperialism.* AK Press, 2013.

West, Cornel. "Cornel West: The Whiteness of Harvard and Wall Street Is "Jim Crow, New Style." Interview by George Yancy. Truthout. March 5, 2021. https://truthout.org/articles/cornel-west-the-whiteness-of-harvard-and-wall-street-is-jim-crow-new-style/.

Wilder, Craig Steven. *Ebony & Ivoy: Race, Slavery, and The Troubled History of America's Universities.* Bloomsbury Press, 2013.

X, Malcolm. "Speech at Ford Auditorium." Speech, Detroit, February 14, 2965. Transcript. https://www.blackpast.org/african-american-history/1965-malcolm-x-speech-ford-auditorium/.

Index

A

Affirmations 263
  Dua for Humanity 263
  Mantras for Enoughness 263
  Mantras for Speaking Up 263

African-ish 77
  A diamond in name 99
  Adopted kin 94
  Africa is feeling 108
  African-ish geographies 81
  African-ish unbelonging 107
  African-ish ways 105
  Apartheid history 86
  Caregiving 96
  Citizen? 80
  Cultural learnings 107
  Debunking African stereotypes 83
  Diamonds worth 106
  Diaspora debates 111
  Diaspora entanglements 112
  Dominant narratives and counter narratives 83
  Embrace humanity 93
  Expat 87
  Global dualities 99
  Heart home 79
  Home-ish 90
  Indians Raced by Apartheid 87
  Indo-Africans 78
  Internalized colonialism 89
  Lost daughter 108
  People create kinship 94
  Postcolonial Africa is a neocolonial Africa, too. 101
  Postcolonialism is a lie 100
  Postcolonial revolutions 102
  Refugees & exiles 95

Scars of love 97
Schooled in saviorism 101
Speaking in tongues 104
Trauma memory 91
Tripod pots 108
Truth & reconciliation history 86
Where are you from? 78
Where we rest in peace 91

american-ish 129
  Abolish America 146
  Academic exiles 156
  Academic unbelonging 153
  america is amerikkka 163
  American racism 161
  Anti-Blackness energies 169
  Black feminists & abolitionists taught me 157
  Brown privilege 174
  Caping & gatekeeping for white supremacy 180
  Cautionary notes 165
  Cultural humility | ਨਿਮਰਤਾ 183
  Defending whiteness 175
  Diasporic grief 193
  Discriminated while degreed 154
  Dismantling is unbelonging 191
  Disrupting harm 176
  Emotional processing 195
  F-1 149
  Fields of study 153
  Global migration crisis 134
  Human dictionary 138
  Humanity of Black folks 179
  Hurt people hurt people 176
  If they come for us, where will we go? 148
  I is for immigrant 139
  Immigrant code switching 142
  Immigrant explanations 141
  Immigrant invisibility 141
  Immigrant misfit 145

Immigrant trauma responses 132
Inquiry is not inquisition 136
Intersections 192
I often exclaim: 134
i/we 182
Karma reckoning | कर्म 183
Multi-faith 166
Multi-identified 160
My american dream 147
My coming to america 130
Nah to white feminism | नही 188
Nazar | نظر | नज़र 185
No chai 181
No denialism 166
Non-white 185
No to cultural appropriation 186
On being an aunty professor 154
Oppressive behaviors we display 171
Othering is dehumanizing 140
Our home 160
Parenting Black children while brown 162
Polycultural 159
Race lighting 177
Re-entry to america 131
Refusal 186
Refuse nationalism 146
Rules of engagement 177
Safe & brave spaces 151
Soul-wounding 165
Spaces & places where I have learned
    & labored 151
Speak belonging 191
Spelling "BE" while Indian 143
Stepmother 167
Together Family | खानदान 167
Truthful reckoning 170
Truths about america for all times 145
Unbelonging is our vibe 161
Ungrateful immigrant 144
What if the marginalized did not marginalize? 182
What is the karma of brown folk45 in settler colonialism? 172

What we are called here: 137
Who is Blindian? Blasian? 162
Words for others 137
Words to signal dominant (white) gaze 184

D

Desi-ish 33
  A note to my aunties from my younger self 47
  Are you? 34
  Boli | ਬੋਲੀ 68
  Chup kar | चुप कर 67
  Desi-ish 34
  Disgraceful desi 50
  Elusive authenticity 46
  Fascist state 63
  Filling in blanks 64
  Head cover, sir dhak lo 43
  Identified by imperialism and colonialism 56
  Identity. Who am I? 36
  Lessons in obedience 46
  Meditations on lateral violence 65
  My name is . . . 38
  My not-so indian self 39
  No watan 56
  Partition–we are kin 58
  Punjabi beti | ਬੇਟੀ 54
  Root truth 55
  Seeing red for kashmir 62
  What if we unbelong? 64
  Who am I? 35
  Who taught me to love hate myself? 50
  घबराहट | Ghabrahat 60
  लोग and दुनिया | ਲੋਕ and ਦੁਨੀਆ 54

E

Emigration 119
  Am I a global citizen? 123
  Consent to enter 123
  Fourth World 126
  Immigration inquisitions 120

No return 127
Re-educated 120
Send us back 124
Where they see me as one of them 122

I

Identities 15
  Are you still at a loss when you are asked identity questions? 18
  Belonging struggle song 23
  Diaspora 24
  How about asking, how do you identify? 23
  Human | رش | इंसान | Humaine 23
  Identity struggle song 19
  -ish? 24
  Naming is healing 22
  Question identity 22
  Symptoms of unbelonging: a self-diagnosis 23
  UnBox Me 18
  What am I? 17
  What is identity? 17
  What not? 22
  Why identify? 16
  Words matter. Names matter. 20
  Words they call me 21

Inquiries for self reflection 261

R

Revolutions 231
  Fight fire with fire 237
  Life working 233
  Peoples' revolutionary movements 236
  Rebellion-Revolution 234
  Revolt | ਰੇਵਲੂਸਨ 233
  Reworking life work 238
  Solidarity politics 236
  Solidarity sayings 236
  Words for liberation 235
  Words for Revolution 235

S

Solidarities 205
   Aatma da kam 224
   A love note to the marginalized maladjusted 215
   Bear witness 213
   Border-free living 221
   Decolonizing is unforgetting 219
   Diasporic potential 209
   Dream decolonial dreams 220
   Honor heritage 214
   Hopeful audacity 218
   How do I center? 211
   Interrupt injustice 212
   Learn anti-racism 211
   Learn languages of liberation 214
   Learn nuance 212
   Liberation praxis | آزادی | आज़ादी 217
   Make new identities 212
   Maladjusted humans 209
   Open heart living 216
   Pyar revolution 216
   Question identity & belonging 208
   Resist dehumanization 213
   Sahaara Aspirations | ਸਹਾਰਾ 224
   Share power 213
   Solidarity is not silent 228
   Solidarity sings 229
   Solidarity stands 229
   Solidarity statements 225
   Solidarity struggles 228
   Solidarity summons 227
   Unbelonging is solidarity 226
   Unlearning is heart work 208
   Unlearn oppression 210
   Unmake this world 207

DIASPORA·ISH

Gayatri Sethi

Inquiries for self-reflection

Who taught me to hate myself?
Who taught me to love myself?

Who taught me to doubt myself?
Who taught me to value myself?

Who taught me to embrace myself?
Who taught me to accept myself?

Who taught me to know myself?
Who taught me about myself?
Who taught me to learn myself?

Who taught me to translate myself?
Who taught me to assimilate myself?
Who taught me that adjacency is belonging?

Who taught me to erase myself?
How did I learn to hide myself?
Who taught me to be my full self?

Whose assessments about myself am I taught to value?
Whose opinions and life experiences are devalued?
How do I define my worth?

Who taught me language?
Who taught me code?
How did I learn the power of language?
How do I apologize for harm?
How do I hold myself accountable for
the impact of my actions?
How do I find space to repair?
Who taught me liberation?
Who taught me revolution?
How do we dream up solidarity?

Who is my community?
How do I create belonging to community?
How did I learn to be in community?

Who is my refuge?
How do I feel safe?
Where is my sanctuary?

What have I gleaned from this book?
What does unbelonging mean to me?

Who taught me how to live?
Who made it possible for me to thrive?

Affirmations

Create your own affirmations for learning and living. Here are a few of mine:

Mantras for Speaking Up

forget obedience.
forget politeness.
unlearn silence.
cultivate confidence.
speak from the heart.
raise your voice if you have to.
blow your own mind.

Dua for Humanity

may other humans grant me the grace
& acceptance I grant them.
may there be space & place for us all
to be humanly human.

Mantras for Enoughness

i affirm
i am a work in progress.
i am enough,
i am more than enough.
it is unbelievable how enough i am.